Community Connections!
Relationship Marketing for Healthcare Professionals

Kelley S. Mulhern, M.S., D.C., M.P.H.

ISBN 13: 978-0-9972263-0-0
eISBN: 978-0-9972263-2-4

Library of Congress Control Number: 2021908660

Sage Media Publishing

Community Connections!
Relationship Marketing for Healthcare Professionals

Whether you're a chiropractor, medical doctor, massage therapist, veterinarian, acupuncturist, or any other provider of a healing art, the healthcare industry is rapidly changing. If you want to connect with your community and achieve greater success, marketing is a must—a fact that has unfortunately been overlooked in many health-related fields of study.

But why don't many independent healthcare professionals tend to actively market their services? And how can self-awareness help you forge a genuine relationship with potential clients?

These questions and more are addressed in Community Connections, a valuable guide full of ideas for marketing your independent healthcare practice effectively and easily.

Dr. Kelley S. Mulhern has spent more than twenty years in the healthcare industry as an employee, business owner, mentor, healthcare marketing consultant, professional speaker, and educator. She hopes this book will serve as a road map for healthcare practitioners working to build the practice and community of their dreams.

Join my e-mail list for special offers:

www.Dr-Kelley.com

Disclaimer:

This book is designed and intended solely to provide information to its readers and is not an exhaustive discussion of the content area. The information is provided with the understanding that the author or publisher are not engaged to render any type of legal, accounting, business, financial, tax or any other kind of professional advice or services. No warranties or guarantees of any kind including those concerning local, state, or professional legality, marketing success, financial growth, or practice growth are expressed or implied. Neither the publisher nor the individual author shall be held liable or responsible to any person or entity for any injuries, losses, untoward results, physical, mental, emotional, financial, economic, commercial, or character damages, including, but not limited to, special, incidental, indirect, consequential, punitive, or other damages which are or are perceived to be the result of any actions taken or inspired by the information supplied in this book. The reader alone is responsible for his or her own decisions, choices, actions, and results. Every healthcare business and practitioner is different and the information and strategies contained herein may not be suitable for your situation. Please consult with an appropriate and qualified legal, accounting, business, financial, or tax professional for advice specific to your situation.

Dedication:

To my husband, Michael, for believing and for "making it happen."

"We never know how far reaching something we may think, say or do, today, will affect the lives of millions tomorrow."

-- B.J. Palmer, *Palmer's Law of Life*

Contents

Foreword

Dr. Kelley S. Mulhern's explanation of how a healthcare provider should relate to his/her community is very timely. Two of the three legs of the concept of evidence-informed care are clinician experience and patient preference. Much has been said about the third leg of this concept, published peer-reviewed literature, and not enough has been talked about the first two legs. In Dr. Kelley S. Mulhern's work, she helps the healthcare provider understand the essential under-pinning of those first two legs -- being connected with a community. It's much more than marketing. It's becoming one with your community, with its heart and soul. It's important to good health that patients feel their doctor or other healthcare provider cares about them not only when they're in the office, but also outside the office.

In previous times, it was said that the healthcare provider was "a pillar of society." He/she was at PTA meetings and involved with children's sports and other activities. The healthcare provider participated in community events, served on school boards, and was involved with professional organizations such as local healthcare associations. In today's fast-paced world, many healthcare providers stay in their office all day and then go straight home at night. They don't develop real relationships with others and rarely make new friendships once they're in practice. There must be a balance between professional life and personal life. Dr. Kelley S. Mulhern shows that to be a truly caring and successful healthcare provider, you must once again become a pillar of society.

Get to know your community and get involved. You will be happier and your practice will boom. People want to feel they're important to their doctor or healthcare provider; that they aren't just another name or account to bring in money. People can tell if their healthcare provider really cares or is, as Dr. Kelley S. Mulhern puts it, an "I pretend to like you because I have to" person. That type of provider must constantly market to troll for new patients to replace the people who realize their doctor is just a face, not a caring person. Connecting with the community, becoming a real person, is what Dr. Kelley S. Mulhern's work is all about. Dr. Kelley S. Mulhern's own vibrant personality comes out in this book. She shows the reader how to become the healthcare provider that all patients want, someone who really cares about them and their world. To those who wish to become a successful lifelong practitioner, this is a MUST read!

Patrick Montgomery, DC, FASA, MS

Associate Professor of Chiropractic History, Philosophy & Technique:
Logan University – College of Chiropractic

President: Missouri State Chiropractors Association

1st V.P.: Association for the History of Chiropractic

Acknowledgments

The saying goes that "it takes a village to raise a child." Likewise, it took a community to prepare me to write this book. Sincere thanks and appreciation are due to so many, and I can't possibly list them all here. For those of you not mentioned by name – you know who you are – forgive me.

First, thank you to my husband, Michael S. Mulhern, for encouraging and pushing me to write this book. You saw it all along. Yes (you can quote me on this), you were right! Thank you for your support, brainstorming, technological assistance, and understanding. Your ceaseless and exhaustive efforts will be responsible for creating an empire!

Thank you to Cree and Suki for putting up with all of the hours I locked them out of the office so I could write, and for insisting I come out to play when it was time for a break. (And thank you to Phoenix and Sasha for teaching me that life is too short not to take play breaks!)

In addition, infinite gratitude goes out to:

My family – Dick, Cindy, Adam and Wendy Stockford. No matter the miles between us, you've always been there, cheering me on. Alex, Cady, and Dex . . . you make my heart smile!

My friends near and far. Your acceptance and support have kept me grounded and focused. Jen Baker, Dr. Adam Bordes, Dr. Clarence Brown, Dr. Stephanie Davoudpour, Michelle Gremillion, and Nancy Pendleton . . . my life would be so boring without you!

My Louisiana family. You've welcomed me into your lives with open arms and are quick to celebrate every success no matter how small. Thank you for making me part of your family!

My teachers and mentors. You may not have realized how impactful your actions or words were to me at the time, but I was listening and watching. Dr. Ron Boesch, Dr. Stu Cayer, Dr. Bill Huber, Dr. Norman Kettner, Dr. Ted Lane, and Dr. Pat Montgomery – you led by example and were excellent role models!

My tireless editor, Toni Poynter Sciarra. Thank you for holding my hand and helping me understand this new industry. Your humor, compassion, and wisdom were evident in every meticulous edit. I look forward to our next project!

Irini Stefa, owner and graphic artist at EyeQCreations, who never complained and reworked our cover image until it was perfect!

The educational institutions, professional organizations, and industry leaders that train and assist healthcare providers. My years at Logan College were some of the best times of my life and provided me with a solid foundation for practice.

Healthcare providers all over the world who give of themselves every day to improve the lives of their clients and their communities. I'm humbled to be your colleague, and I hope this book serves as a resource to help you change the health of those around you.

Finally, heartfelt thanks and appreciation are owed to the multitude of clients, patients, and communities we serve . . . without you, it's all for nothing.

Introduction

If you're a healthcare professional looking for ways to expand your practice and your community, you've selected the right book! Whether you're a recent graduate or a veteran healthcare provider, this book can help you grow your practice, your community, and yourself. Medical doctors, dentists, chiropractors, naturopaths, homeopaths, acupuncturists, energy workers, massage therapists, physical therapists, nurse practitioners, physician's assistants, mental health professionals, and even veterinarians may find resources and information in this book to invent or re-invent the practice of their dreams!

While the health professions are among the most rapidly growing in our society, individual healthcare professionals may remain relatively anonymous bastions of information, help, and support in their communities. Many of us graduate from our respective schools full of hope and optimism, ready to change the health of our communities and the world. However, generally speaking, curricula for healthcare providers historically have included few (if any) courses on business, finance, accounting, marketing and the like. While I'm happy to report that this trend is changing and healthcare schools are beginning to incorporate more business-themed classes into their curricula, we have produced generations of talented healthcare providers who have a great deal of professional knowledge, but who are hampered in delivering it because they don't know much about starting, running, maintaining, and growing a business within a community.

I speak from personal experience. Chiropractic was my second career. (My first career was as a Human Resources Generalist in a family-owned business with 500 employees.) When I graduated Chiropractic College, I was ready to change the health of the nation, one person at a time. I figured that with my experience of working in a large company and my extensive education, my practice would explode in no time. I was wrong. I rapidly realized that, while I was a knowledgeable doctor, I knew nothing about the business of being a doctor. I was desperate for information and spent hundreds of hours in the local bookstore reading books on marketing. Unfortunately, none of them addressed the specific circumstances of marketing for healthcare providers. I began thinking about how the material I was reading could be modified to apply to healthcare, and I started to build my mental list of potential marketing strategies. Six months after graduation, I accepted a position working for another chiropractor who was an accomplished entrepreneur. I was fortunate to have found an excellent mentor early on who helped me to learn some fundamentals of the business of chiropractic. But even with a skilled mentor to guide me, it wasn't an easy road.

Changes in the healthcare landscape have compounded the problem. When HMOs entered the scene, they requested reduced rates for their members and promised that what providers lost in individual charges they would make up in volume. The HMO system virtually eliminated the need for external marketing because the provider had a "captive audience." In the years since, while we've seen some positive changes in the healthcare landscape, we've also seen growing problems:

• Doctors working harder to treat more patients, yet making less money.

• Increasing frustration on the part of providers and patients alike.

• A deepening disconnect between providers and the communities they are supposed to serve.

While the above issues are fairly self-explanatory, let's take a moment to understand why doctors and patients are becoming more frustrated. For healthcare providers, some of the frustrations include the (perceived) insurance company interference regarding the treatment of their patients, the tremendous increase of paperwork, and the plethora of regulatory changes. As a healthcare consumer, you may be able to think of several ways in which the healthcare industry has left you irritated or frustrated. Patients also can be aggravated by network restrictions, coverage or eligibility issues, the length of time they must wait to get an appointment, the decreased time actually spent with the healthcare provider, the increased complexity of navigating the healthcare arena, and the drastic increase of their out-of-pocket expenses. Especially with recent economic events, we're all sensitive to the thought of paying more and receiving less.

The goal of this book is to help bridge the gap between healthcare providers and their communities while increasing the success of their practices. An actively engaged population becomes more health-conscious and health-literate—and looks to the well-known healthcare provider for answers and assistance. As a result, the population becomes healthier, the practice becomes more successful, and the provider becomes more integrated into the community. Everyone wins. While it takes time, effort, and patience to cultivate long-term community connections, it's well worth the investment. Do you remember how excited you felt on your first day of practice? Wouldn't you like to feel that excitement again?

While there's no "magic bullet" for success, I hope this book will provide you with some of the essential tools you need to create a strong, positive connection to your community. One of a series of books on relationship marketing I'm writing for healthcare professionals, this book looks at external marketing strategies and events you can use to forge community connections. The second book, **Practice Excellence!** *An Integrated Approach to Creating a World-Class Healthcare Practice*, continues where Community Connections leaves off. It discusses the additional dimensions of internal marketing and practice management concepts to achieve practice excellence.

In Parts 1 and 2 of this book, we'll explore important fundamentals of healthcare, business, and relationship marketing. In Part 3, you'll find a wide variety of ideas for making external Community Connections, with suggestions for implementing them.

Let's get started!

Part 1:

Where to Begin?

Chapter 1:

Why Don't Healthcare Professionals "Market?"

That's a good question. It's also a trick question—because healthcare professionals *do* market! In fact, everyone (regardless of their profession) markets themselves in some way, shape, or form. The term "marketing" is loaded with negative connotations and stigma. For many people, it has unpleasant associations with sleazy used car salesmen and gimmicks. The reality is that every human interaction involves presenting yourself or your service, product, or idea in a favorable light . . . in a word, marketing! Let's look at some other reasons healthcare professionals may steer clear of marketing.

"I'm Good at What I Do. Isn't That Enough?"

After spending time and money to learn their chosen field, many healthcare practitioners operate under the assumption that the public should flock to them due to their superior knowledge and skill. They may see marketing as "beneath" them or "unprofessional." But in today's information-rich society, "experts" are fairly common. If you're in doubt, simply open the phone book (or do an Internet search) and look up healthcare providers in your area with similar specialties. For most practitioners, it *isn't* enough to be good at what you do. You have to help people understand why they should go to *your* office instead of a competitor's. Don't assume the average person understands what you do. Tell them. How many times have you helped someone, only to have them say they wish they had known about the benefits of your services sooner? For how long did they needlessly suffer because they didn't know or understand your profession?

I remember a time when I was still in chiropractic school and I boarded a plane to fly home for Christmas. During the flight, I struck up a conversation with the passenger sitting next to me, and the topic gradually turned to chiropractic. He stated in no uncertain terms he didn't "believe" in chiropractic. Instead of getting defensive, I simply asked questions. It turned out he had many inaccurate thoughts and assumptions about what chiropractors do. During our conversation, I was able to address some of his misperceptions. In the end, he was amazed by the potential of chiropractic, and by his own ignorance. You see, he was a licensed, board-certified medical doctor. At one point, he looked at me and was clearly upset as he contemplated how many patients he had talked out of seeing a chiropractor. How many of those patients had undergone unnecessary surgeries or had been put on narcotic pain relievers with systemic effects, when a chiropractor's intervention might have been less invasive?

This is one example from one profession, but I'm willing to bet most healthcare providers have had similar experiences. Imagine how different things would have been if someone had had this conversation with that doctor years earlier. Multiply that impact by the hundreds or thousands of people and professionals who don't understand what it is that you do. When considered from this perspective, healthcare providers almost have a duty to educate the public about their profession.

If that story doesn't resonate for you, here's another one. In addition to running our businesses, my husband Michael is a licensed massage therapist. A few years ago, while we were living in New Hampshire, one of the politicians introduced a bill to encourage employment and thus boost the economy. The idea was simple. He proposed a reduction of regulatory and licensing requirements for a variety of occupations, with the idea that more people could then begin to work for themselves as massage therapists, estheticians, et cetera. The New Hampshire Board of Massage Therapists planned a day where local massage therapists would give free chair massages to government officials. While receiving their chair massage, officials also received education as to the licensure requirements and health benefits of massage. At the end, the officials were asked to vote no on the upcoming bill. Astonishingly, the vast majority of politicians had no idea massage therapy is therapeutic and has health benefits other than relaxation. Further, most of them hadn't considered the consequences of allowing untrained people to perform massage. The moral of this story is clear: if people don't understand your profession, it may be vulnerable.

"Yikes—It's Scary."

Yes, it can be scary to put yourself out there. What if people don't like you? What if you're giving a talk and the audience starts heckling you or asking questions you can't answer? What if you make a statement that's incorrect? (Let's face it, even though you may have years of training and education, you're still human.) Fear of rejection and fear of public speaking are two major fears of people in general, and healthcare providers are no exception.

Instead of allowing fear to keep you silent, try to think about marketing in a different way. First, remember that it's natural to be nervous. Second, consider it's virtually impossible to please everyone. No matter what you do and no matter how hard you try, there are still bound to be people who are critical of you. Stop focusing on those few, and refocus on the many people you can affect positively. Imagine the people you meet are excited to see you and hear your information. What if, instead of rejecting you, they welcomed you with appreciation and respect? Who knows? As people ask questions, you might even learn something new in the process!

When I was younger I was extremely shy and terrified to speak in public. Classroom speeches and presentations were nightmares for me. I would tremble and struggle with the words, and my stomach was in knots the whole time. My dad used to tell me I *had* to get over this fear because there are very few jobs in life where I wouldn't have to deal with people. Still, I was a nervous wreck. This lasted until I was in my mid-twenties, and then something happened. I had to defend my Master's thesis. I had been working on this project for the better part of eighteen months, and I was required to prepare a two-hour presentation to be delivered in front of my respected faculty. In addition, the *entire campus* was invited. And on top of all that, if the defense was unsuccessful, my degree wouldn't be conferred. Talk about pressure!

In the end, I think about 25 people showed up. Aside from a few relatively minor technological glitches, everything went smoothly. I was able to answer most of the questions asked of me. The questions I was unable to answer were so specific or inconsequential that no one really cared. I simply admitted I didn't know and moved on. To my surprise, I received rave reviews, and yes, my degree was conferred on schedule!

The lessons I learned from that experience were numerous, but there are a couple that fit with our current discussion. First, my audience didn't have to "like" me in order to understand and appreciate the information I provided. Second, when I made mistakes in my delivery or in what I said, the world didn't end. I just corrected myself and continued. Third, if I could get through this, I felt I could get through anything. And finally, all of the anxiety and fear I had felt leading up to the presentation were unnecessary.

So, gather your courage and your knowledge, and you may be surprised to find that marketing isn't as hard as you think!

"I'm a Shy/Reserved Sort of Person."

Some people are naturally shy or more reserved, but that doesn't mean they can't market. It just means they'll likely be better suited to a more subtle approach. As you will see later in this book, there are dozens if not hundreds of marketing strategies. Not every technique works for every professional. Some people like to host large events, others shine in front of an audience, and still others do best when they're one-on-one. Pick strategies that play to your strengths and that suit you. In so doing, you'll achieve better results. For example, if you're nervous speaking in front of an audience, you could host or sponsor a guest lecturer in your area. This would educate your community and promote your practice without requiring you to be front and center.

"I Don't Have Time."

Effective marketing does take time and planning. However, when people say they don't have time, it's often an excuse to cover an underlying issue or concern. My colleague, Dr. Adam Bordes, once commented that while many people say they don't have the time or money to follow through with healthcare recommendations, he sees it as a problem of priorities. If this treatment or service was going to save a person's child, they would make the time and/or money for it. His point was that if a person understands the necessity or value of something, they are more inclined to make it a priority.

Take a few minutes and imagine two scenarios. First, imagine you put off marketing because you don't feel you have the time. What does your practice look like? How busy do you think you'll be? Can your practice grow the way you want it to? How do you feel about yourself? Second, imagine you have taken the time to schedule and prepare for marketing events in your practice. How does this mental image compare to the first? Under which scenario is your practice more likely to prosper?

"I Don't Have a Budget for Marketing."

Refer to the discussion just above on priorities! As you'll discover later in this book, there are many forms of effective marketing that don't require a large budget. In fact, some require no money at all! Marketing on a shoestring budget is a skill any professional can learn. In today's economy, you can't afford *not* to market! Your budget may dictate that you start small, but you must start!

When I opened my first practice, I had no cash flow. That's right: none. In fact, I think I could have written the book on how to *ineffectively* launch a new healthcare practice, because I did just about everything wrong! I opened my doors in January, 2008, just as the economy was taking a nosedive. I opened my practice in an area where I knew no one. I had a very limited amount of money to work with, and that was it. I had no loan, no back-up, and no rich relative who could float me money if I hit a dry patch. It was truly a sink-or-swim situation born out of necessity.

Yet even in that circumstance, I knew how important it was to market. For the first six weeks, I literally had no patients. However, I had plenty of bills. I had to get word out about my practice! It was a scary, stressful, and exciting time.

So, what did I do? I culled through my mental list of marketing strategies and started with the things I could afford. I went to networking meetings. I hit the pavement and introduced myself to local business owners. I sent letters to companies and schools offering free health workshops. I met tons of people and told them what I was doing. I volunteered for various organizations and forged relationships in the community. Gradually my practice grew. I added new marketing techniques and events as cash flow permitted. When I closed the practice two years later to move with my fiancé to accept a new opportunity, I was well-entrenched in the local business community. I held marketing events regularly. I was often asked to speak at different events, and I enjoyed a solid reputation. If I could build that from nothing in two years, imagine what someone could do with a budget or in an area where they already know people!

"I'm Exhausted Just Running My Practice."

Burnout in the healthcare professions is a real risk. We give so much of ourselves and our energy to our clients, and then we still have to find the energy to run a business. Many providers (especially those new in practice with something to prove) work themselves quickly to exhaustion. Obviously we are unable to provide optimal treatment and service at that point. Just as the air travel safety instructions tell us, we must put on our proverbial oxygen mask before we help others.

What can you do to recharge your batteries? The answer is different for everyone, but here are a few suggestions: Take a nap, go for a walk on the beach, listen to music, plant a garden, enjoy a leisurely lunch, read a book, reconnect with a low-maintenance friend, pursue a fun hobby, go jogging, play with a pet, meditate, take an exercise class, et cetera. Schedule the time into your day if you have to, but make de-stressing a priority!

With the fast pace of the industry and the never-ending paperwork, it's easy to lose the passion and excitement that once energized you. Life is too short to live without passion! Determine what brings excitement to your life and see how it fits with your practice. This can be done in two ways. First, try to integrate your interests into your practice. For example, if you're passionate about children and families, you can structure your practice to focus on those types of clients. If you're crazy about rescue animals, perhaps you can organize a health-related event to benefit a local shelter. Second, do things outside of the office that fuel your passion for your work or for life. For example, attend seminars and workshops that educate, excite, and empower you. Take regular vacations with your family. Volunteer at charities that move you. Life can sometimes be a delicate balancing act, but taking the time to balance work and play is always a sound investment in your future.

"I Don't Know How."

As mentioned, healthcare education traditionally has placed minimal emphasis on business and marketing, so most new practitioners enter their respective fields with no such training. Unless they're lucky enough to have a skilled advisor, they're left to learn marketing by trial and error, which can be time-consuming, exhausting, ineffective, and expensive. How does one find an advisor or mentor? One natural source of mentors is the professors and teachers who taught you your profession. Alternatively, you may look to your employer or business partner. You can hope to stumble across one unintentionally (as I did), or you can take specific steps to find a mentor and develop a relationship with him or her.

It's important to note that few people are fortunate to have one mentor who guides them through all of their challenges. Instead, it's more likely you'll have several advisors or mentors who help you in different ways. This is a good thing. It allows you to see things from multiple perspectives, and it reduces the responsibility of your advisor. For example, maybe a local businessperson takes you under his or her wing to teach you about business finances. You may receive valuable instruction on things like how to read a profit and loss statement or how to select appropriate accounting software. Another mentor may guide the development of your professional skill set. A third advisor may help you figure out insurance billing, and so on. One last word of caution: be aware and respectful of your advisor's time. While advisors and mentors are often generous by nature, you don't want to be perceived as taking advantage of their generosity.

Think for a moment of those people (inside or outside of your profession) whom you admire. What is it about them you respect? What would you wish to emulate? Once you have a list of people, narrow it down to your top one or two choices. If you aren't already personally acquainted with this person, how can you obtain a personal introduction? Do you know someone who knows this individual? From there, invite him or her out to lunch or ask if it might be possible to meet. You could use this time to explain what you're looking for and see if this person might be willing and able to help. If so, make sure to set some ground rules for appropriate time boundaries and communication preferences. You don't want to be a pest or, for example, send text messages if this is someone who really prefers phone calls.

If the person is unable or unwilling to accept the responsibility of being your advisor or mentor, be sure to express sincere thanks for his or her time and consideration. Keep in mind that some people may

22

not be comfortable coming right out and saying no to your request, but may be hesitant or noncommittal. If you get that impression, you may want to respectfully ask if the person would like to discuss any reservations. A little dialogue may clear the way for a successful relationship. If the person is still hesitant, perhaps he or she could recommend someone else you might approach.

Sometimes the best mentors aren't the people who are just like you – they may be people who think differently than you and help you to see things in a new light. They push you outside of your comfort zone and encourage you to stretch and challenge yourself.

Not only is it important to *have* a mentor, it's also important to *be* a mentor. Being a mentor helps you develop your leadership skills, as well as the skills of the person you are mentoring. In addition, you learn a lot about yourself and your profession! You may be a mentor to a student preparing for work in your field, to a new graduate trying to learn the ropes, to your employees, or to people in your community.

Chapter 2:

Do You Know Who You Are?

One of the most important aspects of any marketing plan is self-awareness. It sounds obvious, but without a clear vision of your professional purpose and personality, even the most carefully planned and costly marketing venture can fail. Having a clear understanding of your professional identity is especially important for those healthcare professionals who are employees of other practitioners or those who are independent contractors within an existing practice. In these situations, all of the providers typically use the marketing strategy that works for the owner or lead practitioner. But the owner or lead practitioner's professional priorities and personality may be very different from yours, so their marketing style may not "fit" you. This is common sense, right? Right! But it's surprising how few people realize it.

The concept is really quite simple: **Be You.** No one else can fill your niche. If you know who you are and you live in congruence with yourself and your ideals, the rest will come. You will draw like-minded clients to your door. **Be You.** Don't try to be your mentor. Don't try to be the provider you see on TV. **Be You.** Don't try to fake your skills or knowledge—people can tell when you're not genuine. **Be You.** Enthusiastically and without reservation.

But first, you must know who you are.

Your Practice of Self-Discovery: A Self-Assessment

Whether you're new in practice and haven't spent much time in introspection or you've been in practice for a while and want a fresh approach, here are some questions to start you on your process of "practice self-discovery:"

• **What is your passion?** What do you love to do? Is there a way to infuse this into your practice? For example, if you're a dentist and an avid runner, how can you incorporate running into your practice?

You probably wouldn't try to build a dental practice consisting solely of runners . . . but you could get involved in sponsoring or organizing a running club, 5Ks, triathlons, and become visible in running-related events and social venues.

• **Are you congruent?** If you want your community to look to you for nutritional advice, yet you're 75 pounds overweight and drink soda in your office, can you see how your actions are incongruent with your professional identity? Granted, no one is perfect—not even healthcare providers. We all have areas of incongruence we can work on. Find the ones that have the clearest impact on your professional congruence and see what you can do to make changes.

• **What kinds of clients/patients excite you?** Do you love seeing and treating babies, children, athletes, men, women, seniors, other healthcare professionals, or _____ (you fill in the blank)? Conversely, what kinds of patients make your heart sink when you realize they have an appointment to see you that day? (Let's be honest—we've *all* had them!) If a client saps your energy before you even see them, what does that tell you? Figure out the kinds of clients you love to work with, and then design your marketing strategy to attract more of those people to your practice.

• **What is the image you want to present to your community?** Do you want to be the go-to provider for medical professionals, politicians, or athletes? Would you prefer to be the most sought-after nutritional consultant? How can you foster an image of honesty, integrity, congruency, reliability, or whatever else you wish to project? Make sure any marketing you do aligns with this image. For example, if you decide to pursue a joint business venture with another professional, it's your responsibility to check his or her reputation and credentials. Likewise, if you carry or endorse nutritional supplements or other products, make sure to carefully investigate the products for effectiveness and safety.

• **How do you present yourself and your practice?** Do you take the time to be clean and well-groomed? What does this mean to you and your clients? For example, if you have long hair, some people may think pulling it back is more professional, while others wouldn't care as long it's styled nicely. People have different opinions on the professional appearance of open-toed shoes, jewelry, cropped pants, tattoos, and more. Are your clothes professional, neat, and clean? Again, be aware that different people will have varying opinions as to what is considered professional clothing, and since your practice will probably bring many different people through your doors, it's best to err on the side of caution. Is your practice clean and organized? As you can see, your image extends not just to your presentation of yourself, but also to your facilities and to any marketing materials associated with your practice. Regularly take a fresh look at yourself and your practice. Walk through your facility as if you were a new client seeing everything for the first time. If you see scuff marks on the baseboard, dog-eared magazines in the reception room, or cobwebs in the corners, what does that communicate to your clients? If your brochures or website have typos, grammatical errors, or other mistakes, what message does that send?

• **What is your reputation?** Perhaps you're new to the area or industry and don't have a reputation there yet. If this is the case, you may want to think about ways to transfer your reputation in one area to the new area, perhaps by asking previous clients to write testimonials for you. Alternatively, do you know someone in your new area that would be comfortable introducing you to friends or acquaintances? Or perhaps you have a reputation you don't like. While a detailed discussion of reputation transfer or improvement is outside the scope of this book, there are many resources available on building or improving reputations. Maybe you've worked hard and have a great reputation in your community. Don't take your own word for it. The best way to find out what others think about you is to ask them. Allowing people to provide their feedback anonymously typically generates more honest responses. This can be hard—you may need a tough skin—but wouldn't you rather know if there's a problem you should address? You can verbally ask close friends and your best clients, or you can send a written (or internet) anonymous survey to your clients. Better yet, send the survey to people who came in for a consultation but never came back, or to clients who have left your practice. If you introduce the brief survey with an explanation that you're trying to improve your services and quality and need help, perhaps they'll take the time to fill it out. Not only may you find areas you need to work on, you may also find issues you weren't aware of regarding staffing, partners, location, or procedures.

• **What is the value or worth of your services?** Don't sell yourself short. If you don't value your skills, education, training, and abilities, your clients won't, either. Establish an appropriate fee for each product or service you provide and stick to it. Many healthcare providers keep their fees within ten percent of their state's workers' compensation fee schedule. Alternatively, you could take an informal poll of similarly-skilled colleagues to determine what they charge and set your price accordingly. Finally, you could contact your state association or professional organizations to identify the going rates in your area for similar services.

• **What is your comfort zone?** We have to know our boundaries before we can push past them. What are your limits and why? For example, maybe you don't like public speaking because you gave a disastrous speech in third grade. Isn't it possible that things could be different now? Be creative in taking steps toward personal growth. Perhaps you start by giving small health talks to your friends and family, to your staff, or to your patients. Maybe you create a "do-over" and give a stellar health presentation to a third-grade class. Or maybe you select a health topic within your realm of expertise that people are confused, concerned or misinformed about. Make a professional video of yourself giving a short lecture and post it on YouTube. Step outside your comfort zone and try new things to enhance and support your professional image. For example, *writing* this book was within my comfort zone. However, hiring an editor and preparing the book for publication – exposing my work to the public – was a huge step outside of my comfort zone! I took it one step at a time, hired high-quality professionals to help me along the way, and created a book I'm proud to have written.

• **Ask yourself one final question:** The Master's Circle™ is a large chiropractic practice management company. One of its favorite questions to ask clients is: "If money were no object and you could not fail, what would your dream life/practice look like?" Play with this question—think about it; journal about it; talk it over with a close friend; share it with a mentor and with your partner. Allow yourself to dream big and see the possibilities—and then construct your marketing to help you get there.

When you have a firm understanding of yourself, your practice, and your personality (and, equally important, an understanding of who you are not, what your practice is not, and what your personality is not), you will be less likely to be sidetracked. Without a laser-beam focus, it's easy to dilute your message. You may find yourself trying to be all things to all people, working in a practice that doesn't excite you, and running on fumes. With self-awareness and practice-awareness, advertising fads and marketing gimmicks (such as bait-and-switch presentations or steep discounts) will not entice you, nor will sketchy business opportunities. You'll be able to discern what will be successful for your practice and what will fail. Best of all, you'll have a quiet confidence that will shine through in all you do, marketing and otherwise.

Learning who you are—as a person and as a practicing professional—isn't a one-time event. Rather, the processes of self-discovery and practice discovery continue on a daily basis as you grow and change. They develop with every step you take to improve yourself and your craft. That's why it's so important to *actively* improve yourself. Read books, attend classes, earn certifications, and take other steps to build your experience and refine your expertise. The more you learn, the more you have to offer. And that's why we do this work, after all!

Chapter 3:

Do You Understand Your Communities?

You don't practice in a vacuum. Every healthcare practice must be considered in the context of the communities in which it resides. That's right, communities, plural. Most obviously, your practice is located in a specific geographic community. But there are also the healthcare communities in your area, as well as your own personal community. Knowing where you "fit" can help you focus your energies. Let's look at each of these in more detail.

Geographic Community

Is the area rural, suburban or urban? What are the local demographics (median income, median age, median education level, et cetera)? Given these factors, consider the following questions:

• *What are the healthcare needs of this population?* A geriatric population in South Florida has different healthcare needs than a young family population in suburban Iowa.

• *What healthcare services does this population want?* Baby Boomers may be looking for anti-aging services, while young families are looking for well-baby initiatives.

• *How can you and your practice meet the needs or desires of your geographic community in a way that's congruent with you?* If you're located in an area with a large geriatric population, will you enjoy working with seniors? If that isn't your preference, would you enjoy working with a subset of that population that resonates with you professionally or personally? If you like working with the types of health issues that golfers commonly experience, you're an avid golfer yourself (or both), perhaps you could build your practice around retirees who play golf. Are there other populations in the area you can reach to build a sustainable practice? If not, can you move your practice to an area with a demographic you are more interested in working with?

• *How can you support community wellness in this area?* Can you donate your time to conduct wellness events, lectures, or screenings? Can you work with at-risk populations to develop a wellness program?

• *How can you give back to this community?* Can you serve on the PTA, the school board, non-profit boards, or local government? Can you sponsor charity events? Can you mentor teenagers or young professionals?

• *What are your best networking opportunities within this community?* What relationships do you naturally develop (neighbors, business acquaintances, et cetera)? What relationships can you seek out (for example, other healthcare professionals) to create cross-referral opportunities?

Healthcare Community

What does the healthcare landscape of your location look like? Are there many alternative or complementary providers? Is it largely mainstream allopathic care? How can you support and develop your professional community? Consider the following:

• *How can you support and give back to this community?* Can you serve on professional boards? Can you co-sponsor charity events? Can you mentor new healthcare professionals?

• *What are your best networking opportunities within this community?* What professional relationships can you naturally develop (neighboring businesses, offices that treat similar clients, et cetera)? What relationships can you seek out (for example, other healthcare professionals to create cross-referral opportunities or those providers whose specialties are complementary to your own)?

• *How can you help other healthcare professionals prosper?*

Personal Community

Your personal community can consist of family, friends, neighbors, high school or college alumni, educational alumni networks, professional contacts, and previous co-workers in any industry. These people may be part of your geographic or healthcare communities. But even if they aren't, they might know people where you're located who need your services. Additionally, you might be able to contact your personal community or the people they know with marketing materials.

• How can you best communicate your skills and services to these populations?

• What are their health needs and concerns?

Part 2:

Connecting vs. Marketing

Chapter 4:

Community Connections

Relationship marketing (what I call "Community Connections") is the concept of developing real relationships – not fake "I-pretend-to-like-you-because-I-have-to" relationships – and then leveraging those relationships to benefit everyone involved. It's a slower process that emphasizes education and mentoring. Essentially, you plant the seeds and cultivate growth. In developing Community Connections, often the first question you ask another professional is "How can I help you?"

In Chapter 3, we discovered that all healthcare practitioners belong to at least three different communities: geographic, professional, and personal. Connecting with any or all of these communities can bring personal satisfaction and professional success. Remember, all human interactions contain an element of "marketing," but many people dislike that term because of the negative connotations it carries. Don't beg or manipulate clients to purchase your products and services. Instead, connect with people and serve your community so when your product or service is needed, they naturally turn to you.

In today's environment where people are increasingly disconnected from the human element, many crave a real connection with others. Imagine how you and your practice will stand out in the community if you simply take the time to actively listen to your clients and be genuinely concerned with their well-being. There are many important facets of Community Connection, including relationships and leadership. Let's take a look at each of these:

Relationships

Relationship marketing doesn't mean you have to be every client's best friend. And I hope it's obvious it doesn't mean you should engage in inappropriate relationships with your clients. It simply means treating your clients as human beings – not just as clients. A foundational component of any relationship is respect. It sounds over-simplified to tell providers to respect their clients, but let's take a closer look. Being respectful of your client means:

• **Checking your ego at the door.** This relationship isn't about feeding your ego. It isn't about your intelligence or need to be right. It's about the client – first and foremost.

• **Speaking to them in language they can understand, without being patronizing or condescending.** This might mean avoiding the use of unnecessary medical jargon. It might mean learning to speak another language—literally. Even knowing a little of another person's language can help establish a bond.

• **Educating them as to their health, and then letting go of attachment to the outcome.** This doesn't mean you don't care about your client. However, we must recognize we can't control the actions, behaviors, and choices of our clients. As in a parent-child relationship, we provide a foundation for our clients and hope they make optimal choices. Empower and trust them to make the decisions that work best for them. You may not agree with their decisions, but you aren't the one who has to live with them.

• **Valuing their opinion.** While your clients may not have the education or training you have, they have lived in their body for a long time and know it best!

• **Listening to them.** Actively listening to your client means paying attention to subtle verbal and nonverbal cues. Do you hear or see hesitancy, embarrassment, worry, annoyance, bravado, or fear? Don't go on auto-pilot, tune out, or compose your grocery list while you are supposed to be listening to your client.

• **Giving them your best.** If there are factors (i.e.: personal issues, personality clashes, et cetera) that are negatively affecting your ability to do your best by your client, reschedule your appointment or refer them to another provider.

• **Valuing their time as much as you value your own.** Imagine entering the office of a prominent orthopedic surgeon and seeing a plaque on the wall that reads: "Average wait time: 3 hours." Yes, that's a true story! While it's understandable that every circumstance cannot be foreseen and sometimes people may have to wait, what message did that sign send? It told patients they were not worth the effort it would take to correct the scheduling process to avoid lengthy delays. It told them they and their time were not as important as the surgeon.

• **Understanding their culture and beliefs.** Different cultures have different approaches toward health and healing. Keep an open mind and ask courteous questions if you don't understand a client's culture.

• **Being genuine.** Don't pretend or fake your knowledge, your intentions, your skills, your attitude, or your relationship. As mentioned, people know when you aren't genuine. If you are seeing this client only for the money or for some other form of personal gain, the client can sense that, too.

• **Providing value.** Charge a fair price for your services, do your best by your clients, and strive to exceed their expectations.

• **Connecting rather than selling.** Build your relationship with community members by being respectful, engaged, and professional. When they (or someone they know) need your services, you'll be the first person they'll think of.

For more information about treating patients properly, read *A Patient's Point of View* by William Esteb. It was written from a chiropractic perspective, but the essence of what Esteb is saying can be applied to all healthcare clients.

Leadership

While this has become a popular buzzword over the past several years, that doesn't negate its importance in Community Connections.

There have been thousands of books written about leadership. I urge you to read several that intrigue you or that were recommended by your mentor or other businesspeople you admire. Then go on from there to expand your leadership library. We can't possibly cover all the components of leadership in this section, but some of the characteristics that are important to relationships and community are:

• **Service.** The best leaders are also servants of their communities. They're constantly looking for ways to give back. While they aren't martyrs, they understand the best way to reach their own goals is through helping others.

• **Compassion.** A leader can relate to people on an emotional level and understand the challenges or suffering they're experiencing.

• **Reliability and dependability.** Leaders honor their commitments and can be counted on to keep their word.

• **Honesty and integrity.** See above!

• **Collaboration.** A leader is always striving to help others achieve their goals. Working together with others, a leader looks for opportunities to create win-win solutions.

• **Passion.** A leader's passion for their cause (or profession!) can be contagious! If you don't love what you do, find something else to do. Life is too short to live in boredom or unhappiness.

• **Vision.** People will not follow a leader who doesn't have a clear sense of where they're headed. The vision must be clear and communicated effectively.

• **Wisdom.** While passion is an important feature of a leader, it must be tempered by wisdom. Think situations through carefully and consider multiple sides before reaching a conclusion or making a decision. If you don't possess the information necessary to make a wise decision, confer with someone who does.

• **Skills and knowledge.** Continually improve upon these two elements. If your vision is to lead your community to the lowest obesity rates in the state but you know little about nutrition and exercise, you (and your clients) will not be successful.

• **Game on!** Leaders show up and are ready to go at a moment's notice. For example, be flexible and willing to provide your best care for an acute client who must be worked into your schedule. On a larger scale, be willing to take an active role when you are needed, as in the case of community disasters.

• **Fearlessness.** Leaders don't allow failure (or the fear of failure) to paralyze them. They use each situation as an opportunity for learning and growth. (*Failing Forward* by John Maxwell is an excellent book dedicated to this concept.)

• **Confidence.** Leaders have strength in their beliefs. Put another way, people will not follow a wishy-washy leader. This doesn't mean you should act like a know-it-all, but it does mean knowing what you are good at and communicating your knowledge with calm clarity. If you aren't confident in your education, training, experience, or skill set, do what it takes to develop confidence in your practice.

In his book *Endless Referrals* (McGraw-Hill, 2006), Bob Burg states, *"All things being equal, people will do business with, and refer business to, those people they know, like, and trust."* Developing Community Connections is all about building relationships one step at a time. There are no shortcuts to earning trust and respect. Being a leader in your community provides people with an opportunity to get to know you, to like you, and to trust you. Make sure you're worthy!

Chapter 5:

Marketing 101: The Basics

Branding, ROI (return on investment), product line, strategy, affiliate, B2B (business to business), B2C (business to customer), trending, market-driven, supply and demand, CLV (customer lifetime value), direct response, Four M's, Four P's, influentials, metrics, segmentation, USP (unique selling proposition), consumer, and profitability are just a few common marketing terms. For those of you who are more interested in detailed marketing theory and concepts such as these, you're certain to find some excellent resources on bookstore shelves (as of January, 2021, there were over 60,000 marketing books on Amazon.com). If your eyes started to glaze over just reading that first sentence, have no fear! You only need to know a few marketing terms to get started with Community Connections.

• **External marketing:** This is often thought of as "classic" marketing. External marketing refers to events and promotions held outside of the office setting. Examples: sponsorship of a 5K; attendance at meetings of professional or community organizations; participation in off-site health screenings.

• **Internal marketing:** Internal marketing refers to events and promotions held in the office. It often is geared toward existing clients or even employees. Examples: testimonial contest (explained below), food drive, buy-one-get-one offers, or a movie night in your office.

• **Online/virtual/Internet marketing:** Online marketing focuses on the use of the Internet and social media. (An excellent resource is *Internet Marketing Blueprint for the Fitness Professional* by Dr. Adam Bordes.) Examples: your website; your Facebook page; writing a blog or guest blogging; your use of Twitter and other social media.

• **On-ground marketing:** This type of marketing focuses on traditional physical methods of marketing. Examples: attending networking meetings; participation in the Chamber of Commerce events; handing out business cards.

- **Short-term marketing:** These events have a short time frame for expected results – typically less than 6 months.

- **Long-term marketing:** These events have a long time frame for expected results – typically six months to a year or longer.

- **Marketing calendar:** This is a detailed schedule of all marketing initiatives for at least one year. I call this a Connections Calendar™. More on this in Chapter 6.

That's all of the marketing vocabulary we're going to define in this book! Obviously, there may be overlap between some of these concepts. For example, you may develop an external on-ground event such as a 5K race. Or perhaps you develop an internal online event such as a testimonial contest where clients are entered into a raffle for providing a testimonial about your products or services. The only limitation is your creativity! This book focuses largely on external connection strategies. Internal and Internet strategies will be covered in subsequent books.

Keep in mind that different people may define marketing initiatives in different ways. A friend of mine considers business cards and websites to be internal marketing products, whereas I consider them to be largely external. Sometimes marketing initiatives can be structured slightly differently to make them more internal or external. Don't get too caught up in the labeling. The beautiful thing about Community Connections is that you can customize an idea to suit your community and your practice.

Finally, remember we're all marketing ourselves and our practices. Marketing doesn't have to be distasteful or unpleasant. Effective relationship building can help grow your practice and stimulate success in your life. Be honest, market with integrity, consider the needs of your community, and before you know it, you'll be *connecting* instead of "marketing!"

Chapter 6:

Your Connections Calendar™

Most successful people don't simply stumble upon success – they actively work toward it. Usually they've taken the time to develop a plan and associated goals. For those of you who are groaning and rolling your eyes, this isn't a chapter on how to set goals. What matters is that you set them down in writing and that they be appropriate for your practice. That's what the Connections Calendar™ is all about.

Creating a schedule of connection opportunities need not be overwhelming or difficult. Here are some general tips to keep in mind before sitting down to create your calendar:

• Block time out of your schedule – away from your practice and other demands – around September. This gives you plenty of time to draft, revise, and finalize your marketing plans before the beginning of October. In addition, it provides three months to review your goals and cement them in your subconscious. Has September has already come and gone? Don't use that as an excuse to put this off! Start where you are now, and plan on September dates in the future.

• Depending on your situation, block out one to two full days. If this is your first time making a Connections Calendar™, you may want to give yourself the extra day. Or perhaps you want to update your vision and practice philosophy. Maybe you can use this time as a special retreat where you hole up in a hotel or cabin and focus on you, your practice, and what you want to achieve in the coming year. After you've done this a couple of times, it may only take you a few hours to map out the coming year.

• Have any necessary reference materials and tools readily available. For example, you'll need a calendar you can write on (electronic or paper), a listing of all holidays, a list of all planned vacations for you and your staff, a list of any special dates for your family, a list of potential events and strategies, pens, pencils, calculator, scratch paper, et cetera.

• Bring your "A-Game." When your scheduled time arrives, if you're sick or not in the right frame of mind to get in there and do some serious thinking and playing with your calendar, reschedule your time. But don't be tempted to constantly reschedule – you may never be in the perfect frame of mind. This is a priority and must get done. Think of the time you're spending as an investment in your practice and in your future success, just as important as any class, certificate, or training you take.

• You may want to include other people in the creation of this calendar—perhaps your staff, any mentors you're working with, or trusted friends and family who might have helpful insights. You can include them from the start in all phases, ask them to brainstorm events ahead of time for you to sift through later, or ask for their thoughts once you have created a first draft. While some of these folks will be helping you with these events, remember that this is *your* practice and *you* have to be satisfied with your Connections Calendar™

• Have your creative thinking cap on! Make sure to include new events and opportunities every year. Some events will become your "signature" events—keep those on your schedule—but also add new things to keep your practice and your marketing outreach fresh and interesting.

• If there's an event you really want to do, but you simply don't have the time or other resources, *wait.* Don't set yourself up to fail by taking on more than you can do or hosting an inferior event. If you can't do it right, don't do it...*yet.* But one thing you can do with this year's calendar is to set plans in motion to be able to host that event in the following year.

Eight Steps to Creating Your Connections Calendar™

Now that we've reviewed some general guidelines, let's look at how easy it is to establish your first Connections Calendar™!

Step 1: Survey Your Clients

Prior to sitting down to create next year's calendar, it's a good idea to survey your current clients. Whether verbal or written, this survey can be done in the office or mailed to your clients' homes (or, with their permission, sent via e-mail containing a link to an online survey). It can provide you with specific, helpful information to be used when constructing your plan for next year. Some specific questions to ask:

• Which of our office events or promotions have you participated in over the past year? (You can have them write in their responses, or provide them with a list of events they can check or circle.)

• What were your favorite events or promotions, and why?

• What events or promotions did you not like, and why?

• Do you have any suggestions for additional fun/educational events or promotions you would like to see hosted by this office? If so, what are they?

• If you have an idea to share, please contact the office manager to schedule a time to discuss it. [You may want to offer a small gift to those who give of their time to help you come up with ideas – a raffle ticket, gift card, an ice pack, a book, et cetera.]

Step 2: Schedule Your Events

Go through your calendar month by month and pencil in dates and events from your lists of holidays, vacations, and other important dates. Then start penciling in some marketing events. Hints:

• A good rule of thumb is to schedule one internal and one external event or promotion each month.

• Don't overextend yourself or your staff! It's easy to get carried away and over commit, leading to additional stress and burnout. Start small – you can always add events later!

• Make sure to schedule a variety of events. Doing the same things month after month simply creates another rut. Keep things interesting and new.

Step 3: Set Your Goals

In general, you want to think about a few things:

• What are the results you wish to see from this event (for example: new clients; increased public awareness about a particular health topic; money raised for a charity)?

• Consider the benefits of achieving each goal and the consequences of falling short. This may help keep your motivation high when your energy is low.

• What is the time frame in which you expect to see results from this event? For example, do you want to raise all of the money in a single day? Schedule new clients within one week? Increase awareness of your business within six months? Or what else?

• How will these goals be measured? For example: by the number of new clients scheduled? By the number of new clients who keep their appointments? By the number of new clients who keep their first appointment and are still active in the practice in X number of months? By the amount of money you raised? By a questionnaire to determine awareness of a specific health problem? Or what else?

• Keep your goals do-able. Don't set goals so far beyond your reach that you're doomed to fail. This will result in frustration and lost momentum. On the other hand, don't set the goals so low you could meet them in your sleep. This encourages apathy and complacency. Your goals should make you stretch a little outside of your comfort zone, but still be manageable.

• Are there any particular skills or resources you'll need in order to achieve this goal? Who or what will you need? Will costs be incurred? Have you budgeted for them?

• Now, write those goals down in a handy location! Be as specific and clear as possible. Review them frequently. Break these goals down into component parts (action steps) and enter these steps as appropriate in your Connections Calendar™.

• Take action toward your goals every day.

Step 4: Set Up a Way to Track Results

How will you track the success of your events? You may designate a staff member to do this, but make sure you provide him or her with the necessary tools and information to do a good job. You can set up your tracking format at the same time you create your Connections Calendar™. Below are some ways to track events (you can use more than one!):

• Ask new clients how they heard about you. Actually, this should be standard practice, and your staff should be trained to courteously ask this question when new clients contact your office. This information should be compiled and reviewed to determine what events or initiatives are promoting your practice, and which ones are ineffective.

• A three-ring binder can be used to contain all of your Community Connections materials. It would include:

  ○ A calendar of events with a designated section in the binder for each event.

  ○ The goals for each event.

  ○ A budget for each event.

  ○ Materials created for use in each event (such as flyers, sign-in sheets, PowerPoint slides, certificates, advertisements, and so on).

  ○ An outline of steps taken to bring the event to fruition, along with who was responsible for each step.

○Notes taken in a post-event meeting in which the event is reviewed by the office staff and others who were closely involved. Were the goals met? What worked well? What didn't go as expected? What could be changed for the next time? Are there any loose ends or things to follow up on?

○Any other important information, such as copies of receipts, permits or other documents, client comments, et cetera.

• Instead of a three-ring binder, a digital compilation can be made of the items listed above.

• A goal-specific tracking log can be created. For example, if the goal was to generate new clients, a simple sheet of paper noting the names of the new clients can be used as tracking. While tracking doesn't have to be complicated, it should be thorough enough so you can use the information to streamline and focus your events to maximize your success.

Step 5: Communicate Your Plan

To your staff and to other key individuals who may help you along the way.

Step 6: Execute and Modify Your Event

It's important to build in checkpoints along the way. If the scheduled event isn't going as planned and is consuming tremendous resources (time, money, energy) it may need to be modified. Don't be stubborn and force something to happen – if it's not working, modify it so you can be successful. Again, these checkpoints can be defined as you're establishing your calendar. For example, if you're going to sponsor a 5K but have no co-sponsors or runners three weeks prior to the scheduled event, something needs to be changed!

Step 7: Show Appreciation

Always remember to thank your partners, staff, and participants after each event and after any goal is met.

Step 8: Evaluate Your Event

Did the event go as planned? Did you accomplish what you sought to accomplish? What would you change the next time? Make sure to take notes and put them in a specific place (see Step 4: Set Up a Way to Track Results) for easy access the next time you plan this (or a similar) event. You may think you'll remember, but once you get rolling with Community Connections, you'll have too many things going on to remember all the specifics. Then if you want to revisit or recreate that event, you won't have the information you need to hit the ground running.

Part 3:

External On-Ground Events and Activities

As you explore the ideas for external connection opportunities in this section of the book, keep these notes in mind:

• I hope it's obvious, but the best way to attract and retain clients is to get consistent results. No matter what your marketing strategy, if you can't get results, people won't continue to use your services.

• None of the ideas presented in this book are "new." Rather, they are a compilation of the experiences of a multitude of healthcare professionals over the years, which I've collected in one location for easy reference by practitioners. If I knew a specific individual created a certain event or idea, I tried to give credit for his or her work. If an idea was presented in this book without credit that you can prove was your initial work, please contact me immediately so I can give you proper credit!

• None of the ideas presented in this book are "rocket science." While a certain process or procedure may be unfamiliar to you, most aspects of marketing aren't hard to learn or understand. I've done my best to present information, guidelines, or steps that anyone can follow.

• Not all ideas covered will apply or appeal to all practitioners. In fact, a given suggestion may not be *appropriate* for your practice. Simply take the information that works for you and leave the rest behind. Or you may find that with some adaptation, an idea could work for you and your practice.

• For reasons of space, often only one way to do a particular thing is presented. Realize that it's not the *only* way; it may not even be the *best* way for *your* practice. Use the ideas in this book as a starting point, use your imagination and your common sense, and rework them to fit your situation.

• I have attempted to arrange the events into chapters by average cost:

  ○ Inexpensive ($) = $0 to $500

  ○ Moderately Expensive ($$) = $501 to $2,500

○Expensive or Widely Variable ($$$/V) = More than $2,500 or widely variable

Costs can vary dramatically in different areas of the country. In addition, many of the ideas presented can be executed in a variety of ways, from small-scale to large-scale, which of course can affect the associated expense. Therefore, the rankings in the chapters that follow are just guidelines.

• I haven't presented time commitments for any of these ideas because time frames are virtually impossible to estimate. The amount of time it takes to complete an event or strategy depends upon the scope or level of complexity you choose for the event, your available staff, your personal availability, and numerous other factors. Before you commit to an idea, think about how much time you'll need in order to organize a successful effort. Will you need to engage professional help? Find out who can help, how long they think it will take, and what the cost would be. If staff will be helping, how will that affect the time they can devote to other work in your practice? How much of your own time can you realistically spend? Don't get discouraged; just build in this reality check ahead of time to schedule and scale the event appropriately.

Chapter 7:

Inexpensive ($)

Business Cards

In today's Internet-based society, business cards may seem a bit antiquated. But never underestimate the power of a well-designed business card! Your business card should be clear and easy to read, and it should represent you well. Although online companies may offer inexpensive business cards, they don't send you referrals. A local printer may provide more assistance in designing your perfect card, may mention your practice to others in the community, and you would be supporting your local economy! Be creative – if one local printer tells you something "can't" be done, that may simply mean this particular printer cannot do it. Check with other printers and you'll probably find one who can help you. Some additional tips:

• Don't forget to make use of the back of the business card. You can use this space to add useful information in order to encourage people to keep your card (e.g.: A calendar, an appointment reminder, a list of preventive/wellness tests and when they should be done, or healthy lifestyle tips are just a few examples). Alternatively, you can print an interesting or inspiring quotation about your profession . . . an impactful graphic . . . a funny cartoon . . . a statement of your practice vision or mission . . . or a pledge to your clients, among other things.

• You can be creative in the cut and shape of your business card.

• You can purchase several different designs of your business card in order to have a variety for use in different markets or for different populations. However, be careful not to change the front too much or it can lead to marketing inconsistency and confuse people. (See Jen Baker's comments, below.)

• Do you want special effects such as embossing or a high-gloss finish? Your business card should represent you. What best represents the image or message you're trying to convey? Are there specific standards within your industry? Your local printer can tell you what is "in" and what is outdated. Also consider checking out thermography (to create a raised print) and the use of foil on business cards.

• Consider stock colors other than white to make your card stand out in a crowd.

• Order plenty and distribute them liberally!

Here are several additional tips from Jen Baker, a marketing consultant based in Durham, North Carolina:

• *"A business card is your introduction. It's not meant to be a brochure. A list of services is one thing; a novel is quite different."*

• *"Font selection can be really important. With so many people in the baby boomer years aging, font size needs to be readable."*

• *"Your business card should tie in with the rest of your marketing materials in look and feel. It helps to brand you and make you recognizable. Even if you have several different designs, they should play off a similar theme. For instance, if your colors are green, blue and white, one card can be green, another blue, et cetera."*

Introduction Letter

If you're new to practice or new to an area, you may want to hit the streets armed with an introduction letter and a stack of business cards. You can visit businesses in your community, schedule a time to meet the owners and employees, shake hands, and tell them a little bit about yourself. This is especially important if your profession is not considered "mainstream" or is misunderstood by people. The introduction letter should include your business name, address, and contact information. In addition, highlight relevant experience, skills, and education. In your meetings with other business owners, discuss what sets you apart from other professionals in your field, but be respectful of their time. Ask about their business and what they do, and follow up with a thank-you note. Make certain you proofread and edit your printed materials prior to distribution. You don't want people to remember you by your typos!

Group Memberships

In any geographic area, there are professional, civic, and special interest group membership opportunities. Conduct a little research, ask your friends and colleagues, and select the groups most congruent with your practice style. There may be an initial fee as well as a monthly membership fee, so ask for that information up front. Most groups will allow you to come as a visitor before you decide to apply for full membership. Once you've selected your ideal group(s), consider the time investment. Remember, you don't want to over commit. It may be better to join one group – give yourself time to adjust to the cost and scheduling – and join another group later if you're able. One last caution: these groups should support and interest you. If you find you feel drained after attending a meeting, there's a lot of politics or interpersonal drama, or if the true group goals aren't congruent with your practice, respectfully withdraw from the group or quietly serve out your membership and don't renew. Life is too short and energy too precious to be wasted doing something that doesn't fit with who you are.

The following list of groups is not all-inclusive, but it gives you an idea of the different types of groups you might explore. Larger groups may introduce you to a broader cross-section of industries and people, and they also tend to have more opportunities for leadership positions.

Community Service Organizations

These include Rotary, Kiwanis, Masons, Shriners, Daughters of the American Revolution (DAR), and more. Keep in mind that some of these service organizations may require a recommendation from a current member. In addition, they may have gender requirements.

The focus of these groups is to provide some form of service to their local community.

Leads Groups

These groups, which require a fee for membership, focus on generating referrals and networking. Typically only one person representing a given profession is allowed in each group, so it may take some time for your "slot" to open up. However, be creative! I know one massage therapist who was able to join a group that already had a massage therapist. Instead of promoting her massage practice, she promoted her Juice-Plus™ whole food nutrition business. In doing so, of course, she was able to boost her massage practice.

• **Local:** Local Leads groups may have less stringent membership regulations and policies. In addition, they may be more affordable. If one of these doesn't exist in your area, consider forming one!

• **National/international:** These Leads groups may be larger and more expensive. However, they're organized to promote the success of their members using a framework that has been successful all over the world. Perhaps the most well-known example of an international leads group is Business Networking International, or BNI. (www.bni.com)

Chamber of Commerce

The local Chamber of Commerce can be an excellent source of leadership opportunity, networking, and referrals. Not only do residents of an area look to the Chamber for recommendations, but so do other businesses and companies moving into the area. For example, perhaps a large company is migrating its corporate headquarters to your city. They may look to the Chamber to provide information about medical doctors, dentists, veterinarians, and other healthcare professionals for employees who will be relocating to the area. If you aren't a member of your local Chamber of Commerce, it will be harder for these new residents to hear about you!

Specialty Groups

Every community has numerous groups serving sub-sections of the local population. Finding and joining them can be exciting, as they may align perfectly with your practice. For example, if you're a chiropractor who's passionate about working with pregnant women and new moms, joining a mothers group or the local La Leche League (www.llli.org) would be a natural fit! Some other examples include:

• **Support groups** for families dealing with physical or mental issues. Don't join these groups to "market." Only join these groups if you're passionate about the topic, have a personal connection to the topic, or have a product or service that can truly help these individuals. Serve as a resource for them – don't prey on their distress. Some examples would be support groups for families dealing with autism, domestic violence, Parkinson's disease, Alzheimer's disease, cancer, arthritis, diabetes, stroke, heart disease, emphysema, obesity, and more.

• **Non-toxic living/"green"** groups

• **Exercise classes** such as yoga, tai chi, Pilates, martial arts, aerobics, Zumba, belly dancing, et cetera.

• **Speaking groups:** These groups help you work on your public speaking skills. Not only will you be able to promote your practice more professionally, but you may also make connections with other professionals while attending these meetings. Two examples are Toastmasters (www.toastmasters.org) and National Speakers Association (www.nsaspeaker.org).

• **Professional associations:** It's important to join these associations in order to support your profession on a local and national level. Membership may allow your contact information to be placed in the organization's database and/or on the website, where it can be accessed by other members (who may refer you), or perhaps by the public. In addition, professional groups can provide valuable leadership and mentoring opportunities.

• **Groups based on personal characteristics:** For example, if you're Hispanic, there may be local groups for Hispanic business owners. If you're a young entrepreneur, there may be local groups targeted to your interests and needs. Some examples of specific groups are:

- American Business Women's Association (www.abwa.org)

- National Association of Professional Women, or NAPW (www.napw.com)

- National Association of Women Business Owners (www.nawbo.org)

- Project Eve (www.projecteve.com)

- National Hispanic Business Group (www.nhbg.org)

- Latin Business Association (www.lbausa.com)

- Christian Business Association (www.cbasite.com)

- Association of Christian Businesses (www.tacb.org)

Consulting Services

Never forget you have education, training, experiences, and skills the average person doesn't possess. You can offer consulting services to local businesses in your area(s) of expertise. This marketing strategy can also be a revenue producer for your practice! Only accept consulting opportunities for topics in which you're an expert and that fall within your scope of practice. Some potential topics that may be popular with local businesses include:

- Workplace ergonomics

- Developing an Employee Wellness Program

- Stress management

- Health literacy

- Nutrition (especially if there's a cafeteria on-site)

- Creation of a Health/Wellness Fair

Health Screening or Service

Free local health screenings or services provide an opportunity to educate and serve your community as well as provide value. Depending upon your specialty, the screening may take several forms:

- For chiropractors: spinal screening, posture analysis, or backpack safety screening

- For massage therapists: muscle/movement assessment or 5-minute chair massage

- For dentists: TMJD screening, flossing technique demonstration or oral cancer screening

- For acupuncturists: tongue or iridology assessment

- For MDs, DOs, NDs, et cetera: blood pressure or cholesterol screenings

- For mental health professionals: stress screening

Be creative! If all of the other dentists in your area are offering temporomandibular joint dysfunction (TMJD) screenings, do something different! Think about all of the education and training you have that the average person does not. What quick and inexpensive assessment can you perform that would be beneficial for others' long-term health?

Presentations (One-Time or Recurring)

While many practitioners consider a one-time presentation to be a "waste of time," you never know where that presentation may lead. Perhaps the CEO of a major local company is in the audience and decides she wants you to do monthly "Lunch 'n' Learns" for her staff. Perhaps the wellness coordinator of a local school is present and wants you to be involved in the school system's Wellness Curriculum. A single presentation may lead to increased business, more networking opportunities, and future presentations. If given the opportunity, do it! For those of you who are comfortable with public speaking, don't wait for the opportunity to present itself—create it! Some tips to get you started:

• Depending on your comfort level and experience, you may donate your time or charge a fee. Whatever you choose, make sure it's clear to the host organization.

• Ask your current clients and business acquaintances for opportunities to speak within their business. Better yet, provide them with a list of lectures you've developed for them to select from! (Please refer to Appendix A for a sample list of presentations from one chiropractor's office.)

• Take initiative and create a panel discussion to hold at your office, the local library, or at another local business. Inviting other professionals to be on the panel is great networking, builds professional goodwill, and develops your visibility as a leader in your community.

• DON'T BAIT AND SWITCH!!! In other words, don't agree to talk about a certain topic, but only briefly mention the topic and instead spend most of your time on another topic—or worse, try to hard-sell your professional products or services. This gives you and your profession a bad reputation. Deliver what is requested.

• Practice your presentation until you're comfortable, but not to the point where it sounds memorized.

• Start on time and end on time. It's important to respect and value the time of your participants.

Before the Presentation

Ask the hosts/organizers about their goals for the presentation. If their goals are unreasonable or don't match your topic, discuss modifications both of you could make that would result in a better match between their goals and your presentation. Having this conversation in advance helps demonstrate that their interests are your top priority, and this can help you to create another Community Connection. In addition, clarifying their goals can help ensure the success of your presentation. Meeting or exceeding the expectations of your host can help you turn a one-time presentation into a repeat event. A little planning can go a long way.

Most places – businesses, libraries, schools, or organizations – will have a time limit for your presentation. Make sure you know what this is in advance and prepare accordingly. For your more popular topics, you may want to create presentations of varying lengths— perhaps 30-minute and 60-minute versions. You should also have a high-tech and a low-tech version allowing you to deliver the material with or without projectors, computers, Internet access, or other technology.

Discuss presentation requirements with your host to make certain you have everything you need. Do you need a projector, a dry-erase board, a flip chart, markers, a microphone, a podium, a chair, or anything else to facilitate your lecture? If so, are you responsible for bringing it with you, or will it be provided by your host?

In addition to discussing your presentation requirements, find out in advance what the limits are on self-promotion. Most hosts will understand that you're giving the presentation as a marketing event. Ask if you can mention your practice name, hand out business cards, schedule appointments, or do other things to help market your services. Will you be able to video record the session and post clips or the full presentation on your website? What is acceptable to the host in lieu of payment? Alternatively, perhaps some information about your training, your practice, and how to contact you can be included in the host's introduction.

During the Presentation

Use an *appropriate* icebreaker to help you and your audiences get comfortable. I often begin my presentations with a question, mini-survey, or a moving story to engage and interest the audience. Avoid using humor as an icebreaker because it's very subjective. What you consider to be innocent and funny may offend or irritate your audience.

Take five minutes at the beginning of your presentation to explain your background. This is not about satisfying your ego or grandstanding. Very simply, your audience should know *why* they should listen to *you*. Be brief and mention relevant education, training, experience, and skills. Another option, if your host would like to welcome the group and introduce you, is to have your host offer these details about you—something you can arrange together as part of planning the event.

Next, provide a brief overview of what you're going to talk about. This helps participants put the discussion in context and mentally prepare to receive the information. At the end of the presentation, provide a brief summary of what was covered. Your summary can help participants remember the important take-home points of your presentation.

Again, be prepared to go high-tech or low-tech. While technology such as projectors, computers, and PowerPoint slides is great, if your technology fails, you don't want to be unable to deliver your presentation. Be capable of conducting your presentation with or without technology.

In the midst of the presentation, be entertaining while being educational. Don't speak in a monotone. Provide interesting and relevant examples. Ask for audience participation. Use props or music where appropriate. Don't let your audience fall asleep or feel like they just wasted an hour of their lives! If you're using handouts, don't inundate your audience with them, as too many handouts can distract people from focusing on you and your presentation. Some tips for effective handouts include:

• Create appropriate and clear handouts. These should include any take-home messages you want to be sure your audience leaves with.

• Make sure your contact information is clearly printed on each page.

• If appropriate, insert a copyright line on each handout so it's clear the printed content belongs to you. (Copyright © [insert year] by [insert name])

• Often interactive handouts with blanks that attendees can fill in are effective. The audience must pay attention to the presentation in order to fill in the blanks and have a complete handout. For example, if you're talking about nutrition, one of your handouts might read: "Fat-soluble vitamins include A, D, _____ & _____." By listening to the lecture, the participant would fill in "E" and "K" to have a complete handout.

Not all presentations are perfect, but don't let them see you sweat. Remember, *you* are the expert. If someone challenges you or asks a question you don't know the answer to, handle it with grace and dignity. You might say something like, "Wow, that's a great question! I'm not sure of the answer, but I'm really curious! Let me go back to the office and find the answer for you – shall I call or e-mail you the results?" Admitting you're human and don't know everything can help defuse a tense situation. However, use that technique with caution. You don't want your audience to perceive you as anything less than an educated and experienced professional. Sometimes people have their own ideas to share, and if the subject lends itself to audience participation, you could reply, "That's an interesting thought/question . . . what do you think?" Or you could open it up to the room: "That's an interesting issue/observation. Has anyone else had this experience? What do you think?"

At some point in the presentation you should incorporate a "call to action." This may be as simple as having participants brainstorm and write down how they'll use the information gained from the day's seminar. Or it may be asking them for their business, perhaps along the lines of: "If you'd like to know more about _____ and how it applies to your particular situation, I hope you'll contact me to set up a consultation" as you show your final slide containing your contact information, or as you direct them to your contact information on your handout. In general, an informative seminar is good . . . but a seminar that encourages participants to change is better. Make it easy for them to leave the room with a different mindset than when they entered.

Keep in mind that not all participants will be ready or willing to jump on board and hire you to help them make health changes. If participants leave the presentation with some good information they can apply in their lives, great! That alone may inspire them to share your name with someone else, creating another Community Connection.

Near the end of your presentation, make sure to leave ten to fifteen minutes for questions and comments. You can also use this time to ask participants to complete a post-presentation survey. This survey should be brief and build in opportunities for you to come back! (Please refer to Appendix B for a sample post-presentation survey.) Here are a few simple questions to include, with options for selecting "yes," "not sure," or "no," and to write in comments as appropriate:

• Did you enjoy today's presentation?

• Did you learn something new in today's presentation?

• Do you have any comments, suggestions, or questions about today's presentation?

• Which of the following topics would you be interested in attending a presentation on (check all that apply)? [Here you would provide a list of nine to twelve other health topics for which you've already developed lectures. Also include a space for write-in topics.]

Finally, end your presentation on a positive note, and always remember to thank the audience for attending, as well as the organization and the individuals who made your presentation possible.

After the Presentation

Follow up with a quick thank-you note to the event organizer. If you have survey results to share, you could promise to send them shortly, and then make sure you do. That can also be your opportunity to suggest another presentation, based on the interests expressed by the respondents!

When sending survey results to the host company or organization, do so in summary form. This allows you to provide important information for the leadership team while protecting the anonymity of individual participants. For example: 15 out of 17 surveys were returned. Of those, 14 enjoyed today's presentation, and 1 was not sure. 13 learned something new, 1 did not, and 1 was not sure.

Share any written comments, suggestions, or questions from participants exactly as they were presented. Don't edit them. Finally, share the suggestions received for future presentations. For example: 16 out of 17 would like to attend a presentation on goal-setting for fitness, 13 out of 17 would like to attend a presentation on non-toxic cleaning solutions for the home, and 10 out of 17 would like to attend a presentation on building natural immunity. I'm available the week of [INSERT DATE] to present a goal-setting workshop. Please let me know if this would be of interest, or whether you'd like to see one of the other topics developed. If so, what day and time for this presentation would work best for you?

Create Community

Have you ever felt all alone in your endeavors as a health practitioner? Sometimes it seems the harder we try to help a person or a community, the more resistance we encounter. It can leave you feeling helpless, alone, defeated, and deflated. It's easy to get beaten down by the insurance companies, the "competition," the uninformed public, and even yourself. Feeling this way makes it harder to make an effort to keep putting yourself out there in the larger community, as well as to create community among other healthcare professionals. We need to understand and support each others' professions in order to build Community Connections. If the opportunity to meet, network with, and support other health professionals doesn't exist in your area, create it. Here are some options for professional community:

Mastermind Group

This is a group of others in your profession who meet on a regular basis to share challenges, successes, and ask for feedback. Although this term has been around for decades, I was first exposed to the concept by The Master's Circle™, a chiropractic practice management company. They promoted the groups as a way to provide support to their members between regional seminars by encouraging members to connect with one another. However, members of any profession can adopt the concept of Mastermind Groups.

Basically, here's how Mastermind Groups work. The chiropractors in a given area who belong to The Master's Circle meet once a month, rotating locations to allow everyone a chance to host the meeting. Refreshments are optional. The format is relaxed and simple, with the chiropractors meeting in one room and their staff members in another, so everyone can speak candidly about their respective issues. Each group member shares a recent challenge and how they worked through it or whether they need assistance. Then they share a recent success. There's always time left for questions such as: "I noticed the coding for Blue Cross Blue Shield (BCBS) has changed—how are you handling that?" Or "We're looking for a new receptionist. Does anyone have any resumes they can forward?" Alternatively, the chiropractors and the staff can be in the same room, which can promote transparency and mutual problem solving.

While this format was discussed for chiropractors, it can certainly be adapted for use by other health professionals. Here are the main action points for getting started:

Before the Meeting

- Schedule the location, date, and time.

- Develop a list of potential attendees within your profession.

- Invite participants via letter, phone call, or e-mail.

- Confirm who will be taking minutes and make sure he or she will bring any necessary equipment (a laptop or pen and paper, for example).

During the Meeting

• Have a sign-in sheet.

• Begin the meeting by having each person introduce him- or herself, followed by each person sharing challenges and successes.

• At the end of the meeting, schedule the next location, date, and time if it isn't standard (i.e.: The second Tuesday of the month at 7pm).

• Wrap-up, conclusion, and thanks to all of the participants.

After the Meeting

• Follow up on any action items.

• Distribute meeting minutes.

Practitioner's Circle

Many thanks go to Jeremy Werner, licensed acupuncturist in Arizona, for this idea. A Practitioner's Circle is a group open to *all* healthcare practitioners – whether they work with people or with animals. The goal is to support those who work in health and wellness. The group meets once a month to provide support and a place to network within and across disciplines.

In Jeremy's group, attendees introduced themselves one by one to the group and shared briefly about their profession. (Depending on the size of the group, each person may have 30 seconds to 10 minutes for an introduction—you decide!) Once the introductions were complete, anyone who had a specific issue was asked to speak. The issues ranged from needing someone to proofread and provide feedback on new marketing materials, to needing encouragement after a particular challenge, to asking for help in figuring out additional treatment options for a client's problem. Not everyone will have an issue to address in every meeting. Therefore, each meeting focuses on the practitioners with the greatest need.

While the logistics of a Practitioner's Circle meeting are very similar to those of a Mastermind Group meeting, here are some key points:

• A Practitioner's Circle is not limited to one person per profession. The more, the merrier!

• Don't limit yourself geographically in setting up your Practitioner's Circle. Depending on your area, people may be willing to drive an hour or two for this sense of community and connection.

• Practitioner's Circles can include many different types of health professionals. You may consider including acupuncturists, chiropractors, massage therapists, physical therapists, medical doctors, osteopaths, naturopaths, homeopaths, veterinarians, dentists, mental health professionals, energy workers, Ayurvedic practitioners, intuitives, mediums, nutritionists, personal trainers, fitness professionals, organic farmers, food co-op members, to name some to get you thinking!

Invite a Practitioner to Lunch

This is a very simple, one-on-one way to learn more about other healthcare professionals' businesses. Just contact a practitioner you'd like to get to know professionally, extend an invitation to lunch, and enjoy casual conversation. Ask questions about what he or she does, practice structure, and ideal client, so you have a better idea of appropriate referrals. Talk about your practice and your ideals, and ask for referrals.

Lady Docs

One female doctor, practicing in an area dominated by male doctors, reached out to other female doctors of all types. They met once a month at a different restaurant to network, connect, laugh, and support each other. The social setting provided a relaxed and informal tone that helped the women get to know each other on a personal level as well as share their professional experiences and perspectives.

Volunteer

There may be no better way to *connect* with your community than to *serve* your community. If you look around, you'll find many volunteer opportunities in your area – and one of them is certain to resonate with you. Here are some ideas:

• Serve on the board for a local non-profit organization.

• Work on a planning committee for a charity event or fundraiser.

• Build a house with Habitat for Humanity.

• Handle calls at a local crisis center.

• Provide health screenings for the homeless.

• Deliver food to the hungry.

• Be a Big Brother or a Big Sister.

• Mentor a young adult or a young professional.

• Be the team doctor for a youth sports team.

• Coach a youth sports team.

• Read to the elderly in a nursing home.

• Clean up the environment.

• Donate your time or services to the local Fire Department, Police Department, and EMS. These groups do so much for our communities.

• Donate your time or services to veterans of the armed forces.

• Provide classes to those in a battered women's shelter – topics could include life skills, budgeting, communication, goal-setting, self-esteem, interview skills, and more.

• Work with animals at a veterinary clinic or in a shelter, providing massage, acupuncture, Reiki, or other assistance.

• Serve in the PTA at your child's school

Sporting Events

Local sporting events can range from youth ("Pee Wee") softball games all the way up to adult recreation leagues and professional teams. There are many ways to develop a relationship and promote your business through sporting events. You may sponsor a local team, coach a team, provide game-day medical assistance, or be the team physician. Tips for getting started:

• Select a sport in which you have personal interest and experience.

• Go through proper channels to solidify your relationship. ("Proper channels" will differ depending upon the sport, the venue, the level, and so on.)

• Clarify in advance if you can announce your affiliation with the team. If you're a sponsor or a coach, the answer is obviously yes. If, however, you're the team physician, there may be HIPPA (Health Insurance Portability and Accountability Act of 1996, issued by the U.S. Department of Health and Human Services) issues to contend with.

• Make certain you're clear as to the team's expectations of you. If you're unable to meet their demands (due to scheduling conflicts or other issues) let them know as soon as possible.

• If you're rendering medical assistance in any way, check with your liability insurance carrier to see if additional riders to your policy are needed.

• Maintain professionalism at all times! Never forget that even though this is your personal time, your actions will still reflect upon your practice. For example, if you're coaching a Little League team and a parent starts yelling at you because of a perceived slight to his or her child, don't yell back. Be calm and respectful.

• Document as required any interactions with and/or treatments of the athletes.

• If you're not a physician, you can still provide game-day services. Perhaps you can provide chair massage, assist in triage and evaluation, provide kinesiotaping, or offer facilitated stretching. Be creative and make the case for how your presence could benefit the athletes!

Chapter 8:

Moderately Expensive ($$)

Brochures

Brochures provide an easy, portable way to educate your clients and your community. They may contain information about common symptoms, treatments, or conditions. You may leave brochures in your office, available for clients to read and take with them, or you may hand them out at marketing events. Keep in mind all of the information provided earlier about business cards – the same rules apply to brochures. In many healthcare professions, there are companies who produce high-quality, fully researched brochures for a reasonable price. Look around on the Internet and find a company whose messages are consistent with your practice. Consider some of your most frequently asked questions, and obtain brochures to address those questions.

Alternatively, you may opt to design and print your own brochures. Be careful! If you make your own brochures, do your research! If you make a statement that isn't considered to be "common knowledge," you must cite your reference. If you use information obtained from another location, you must cite your reference. Otherwise you may be guilty of plagiarizing. If you're uncertain if something qualifies as "common knowledge," err on the side of caution and provide a reference. Just because you make your own brochures doesn't mean they can look unprofessional. (Consulting with a local printer or graphic designer can be another opportunity to build a relationship and generate referrals!) Brochures – whether created in your office or by a professional – should be accurate, clear, uncluttered, easy-to-read, free of typos, and informative.

In addition to brochures about symptoms, conditions, and treatments, create an office brochure. It should contain basic practice information such as the name of your practice, contact information, address, office hours, and a brief description of who you are and what you do. If there's room, you can include a list of services, or some FAQs. Break up the text with professional pictures of your office, your staff, and/or yourself.

Awareness Events

Awareness events targeting specific populations such as the elderly, children, or diabetics can be large or small; in your facility or at another location. They can involve other vendors or just your office. One popular awareness event hosted by chiropractors is called Kids Day America™ (KDA). The event was founded by Drs. Theresa and Stuart Warner with the aim of having a specific day every year where chiropractors and their communities across the country focus on children's health and safety. To participate in KDA and use KDA's logo and other materials, chiropractors must pay a fee to KDA and agree to KDA's rules and regulations. Typically hosted in the spring, KDA events facilitate health screenings and the creation of child identity cards. This way, if a child goes missing, the parents have an up to date and accurate record of identifying information to give to law enforcement. Other professionals invited to participate may include:

• Fire department: Firefighters can bring a smokehouse to show the kids, hand out coloring books, and more. The fire engines are on-site, and firefighters take kids up in small groups to explore.

• Police department: Officers can take fingerprints for the child identity cards.

• Photographer: A photographer can take the child's picture to put on the child identity card.

• Dentist: A dentist can do a brief dental check to indicate dental information on the child identity cards.

• Optometrist: A vision check can be educational and fun.

• Chiropractor: A chiropractor may do a spinal/scoliosis screening, backpack safety check, or wellness presentations.

• Massage therapist: Chair massages for kids and parents are beneficial and relaxing.

• Pediatrician: Pediatricians can enter a child's height, weight, and any distinguishing marks or features on the child's identity card.

• Doula, midwife, and/or lactation consultant: These professionals can provide valuable information.

• Local natural food store representatives: They can share information on healthy eating.

• Poison control representatives: They can provide life-saving information and resources.

• Videographer: A short videotape each child captures dynamic images of the child that can be useful if a child goes missing.

• Face painters/clowns: These folks provide entertainment.

At the beginning of the event, each child and parent is provided with a goodie bag and card stock ID card at registration. They proceed to visit each station – learning about children's health, wellness, and safety – until their ID card is complete. There may be door prizes and raffles or other giveaways. All profits (generated by sponsorships and donations) are donated to a local children's charity selected prior to the event. Make sure to alert your local radio and TV stations, as they may want to cover the event as a human interest story.

Another awareness event your practice could host is similar to KDA but on the opposite end of the chronological spectrum: An Elder/Retiree/Baby Boomer Day. Instead of focusing on children's health and safety, the event would focus on the special health and safety concerns of those over 65. This would be a great event in areas where there's a large population of retirees or if your practice has a large geriatric client base. If hosted in an assisted living facility, elder ID cards could be made for the facility to keep on file in case the resident goes missing. Again, make sure to alert your local radio and TV stations, as they may want to cover the event as a human interest story. Let's look at some general steps to hosting an awareness event:

Before the Awareness Event

Select your awareness theme and associated charity. This can be done by you or by popular vote in the community. Determine the format of this awareness event. Would lectures, demonstrations, or literature work best to get your message across? Decide what you want the event to look like so you know how much time to plan, what type of venue to book, and what types of sponsorships, donations, and vendors to solicit.

Next, select the date, time, and physical location of the event. Consider issues such as: Are permits necessary? (If you're not sure, check with your Town Hall.) What are the associated expenses? Who's responsible for setup and cleanup? What items are included at the venue – tables, chairs, microphones, projectors, et cetera? Will there be access to power, water, restrooms, phones, or other necessary items? How will the tables be laid out? Who will be at each table?

Determine sponsorship levels and fees, if any. Ask local businesses for donations or sponsorships. These can take the form of money, donated services, door prizes, tee shirts, or supplies. When asking for donations, remember to be polite. Don't harass people if their answer is no, and show appreciation and gratitude if the answer is yes. Remember to keep track of whom you've called so businesses don't receive multiple requests from your office. One important suggestion: If you have the time, you may send a letter in the mail *prior* to your phone call. This allows the company to think about your request, read about your event, and expect your call. Sometimes companies will call *you* with their donation shortly after receiving the letter!

In addition to finding sponsors, ask other related businesses to participate as vendors or speakers for the event. Be clear about your expectations and what they're allowed to do. If you're charging vendors a fee, be up-front about it. Once your list of vendors is complete, create a floor plan and a schedule of events. Confirm vendors at least one week prior to the event and answer any last-minute questions. Encourage sponsors and vendors to provide handouts or other giveaways to participants.

In addition to scheduling vendors and sponsors, make sure you have plenty of help. Locate volunteers to assist before, during, and after the event. Obtain everyone's contact information, as well as information about their availability. Make "Event Staff" tee shirts in neon colors for your volunteers so participants needing assistance can easily identify staff at the event.

Prepare all event-related materials. Work with a local graphic artist to develop the event logo/image and advertise your event to local businesses, your clients, and the general community. If this is a charity event, ask if the graphic artist could donate his or her time and services. Depending on your budget, event advertising can be accomplished via posters, flyers, e-mails, TV or radio commercials, Facebook, Twitter, or other creative formats. Don't forget to feature the event on your website and on community calendars. Also prepare registration forms, goodie bags, presentations, handouts, and anything else that may be used during the event.

During the Awareness Event

On the day of event, ask vendors to arrive at least one hour early to set up. Check for any unforeseen issues such as power and supplies (the amount of voltage, the availability of physical supplies like cables, location of power outlets, sufficiently long extension cords, adaptors, and so on), not enough seating, et cetera. Make sure your volunteers are wearing their neon Event Staff tee shirts and that they have everything they need. Check in periodically with all vendors and staff. In general, keep things running smoothly and on time (if applicable). With appropriate planning, you should be able to relax and enjoy the event!

After the Awareness Event

Follow up with thank-you cards to sponsors and vendors. Contact local media for coverage on the funds raised or other outcomes of your event. Debrief with volunteers, staff, sponsors, and vendors to see how the event could be improved next time. Organize a file or folder with all event documents and information to use as a starting point for future events.

Smaller-Scale Awareness Events

You can host a health awareness event easily in your office. Check http://www.national-awareness-days.com/ for a comprehensive list of health awareness months and recognition days. Simply select one and build your event. For example, April is stress awareness month. You could host an informational session in your office with mini-presentations on specific topics and samples of appropriate products. October 6th begins National Midwifery Week. If your practice focuses on pregnant women and children, this would be a perfect fit! You could have one event or a series of presentations and workshops all week long.

Awareness events take time, effort, and planning, but they can be well worth the investment. There may be a bit of a learning curve on the first one, but after you've done it once, subsequent events are much easier. In addition, hosting a large event can help to brand your practice in the community. Businesses and individuals begin to look forward to that event every year. It feels great when local companies start building a donation to your charitable/awareness event into their annual budget!

Collaboration

Unfortunately, many business owners become territorial when marketing their business, and healthcare professionals are no different. I've heard this phenomenon explained in terms of a pie: healthcare professionals are all looking for their piece of the pie (meaning more clients). However, if we team up and educate our communities, the "pie" (market base) becomes bigger, allowing for more "slices" (market shares). There are more than enough clients to go around. Instead of competing with other healthcare professionals, look for ways to foster professional collaboration and raise public awareness of health issues. Here are some ideas:

• Host joint events: For example, co-sponsor a local 5K or other charity event.

• Dive into a long-term project together. For example, co-create a Wellness Program for a special population/profession which draws on both of your skills and talents.

• Team up with other professionals to bring an amazing speaker to town for your clients and the community.

• Be a guest speaker for each other's events.

• Guest-blog for each other

• Create a joint blog, monthly community lecture, newsletter, or radio show.

• Share marketing materials such as PowerPoint presentations.

• Combine your complementary areas of expertise to write a book together.

• Create or join a Mastermind group.

Write a Book

In today's world, self-publishing technology lets us put our ideas into print. All it takes is a computer, the Internet, some time, some knowledge, and a passion to communicate with others. Your book doesn't have to be tremendously long and difficult to do. Sometimes the hardest part is simply starting—sitting down and putting words on paper. (It took me almost ten years to sit down to write this book . . . and less than two months to actually write it!) Commit the time. Take action. The rest will follow. Once you have written and published the book, it can be promoted on your company website, on your business cards, and anywhere else you promote your business. It can even serve as a way to get people on your mailing list. You've probably visited websites where you're asked to enter your name and e-mail address for a free newsletter or to join a mailing list (i.e., opt in) in exchange for a free download. Once people have opted in to be on your mailing list, you can send them newsletters, notices of upcoming events, and specific health information.

If you're interested in writing but aren't confident about your skills, I would recommend Stephen King's book *On Writing*. Yes, the father of horror has written a nonfiction book in which he interweaves his personal story with tips and suggestions for novice writers. It's an excellent resource. If grammar isn't your strong suit, make sure to have a copy of the legendary *Elements of Style* by Strunk and White. For a comical look at grammar, try *Eats, Shoots & Leaves* by Lynne Truss. For accurate information regarding industry standards pertaining to book writing, formatting, editing, and publishing, look to *The Chicago Manual of Style, Sixteenth Edition* by the University of Chicago Press. (I'll tell you a secret: all four of these books are on my desk as I write these words!)

You may write your book by yourself or in collaboration with another professional. (Just think – that means twice the information and twice the exposure!) You can write about a specific health concern (such as arthritis, scoliosis, diabetes, cancer, or heart disease), a specific health solution (such as diet, the glycemic index, exercise techniques, spinal decompression, herbal treatments, or supplements), or a specific health profession (such as acupuncture, chiropractic, massage therapy, physical therapy, or homeopathy). You may choose to combine one or more of these for a comprehensive approach.

No matter your topic, make sure that you understand what message(s) you're trying to communicate, and to whom. Who is your target audience? If your audience is your client base, then you wouldn't write a book loaded with medical terms easily misinterpreted by the layperson (or if you used medical terms as part of helping to educate your readers, you'd want to make sure you defined them). If your audience is other healthcare professionals, you could use medical terms more freely.

Create a space where you can work comfortably. Have an appropriate desk, chair, and the ability to close the door so you aren't interrupted. Make a habit of writing: go to your writing space at the same time every day, sit down, focus, and write. It doesn't have to be perfect the first time. Just get the information down on paper (or on-screen) and revise it afterwards. *need* What are you waiting for? People the health information you have in your head – provide it for them.

If you don't have time to write a book or if that feels too daunting right now, consider writing a series of one-page articles to post on your website or print in high-quality form and offer as giveaways in your office. Or write a white paper—a longer piece on a specific topic—and offer it on your website or to clients. Once you get in the habit of writing and improve your writing skills, you may find the idea of writing a book more appealing.

Lastly, I offer ghostwriting services where I write the book for you and YOUR name is the author. Please contact me directly at drkelley@dr-kelley.com.

Chapter 9:

Expensive or Widely Variable ($$$/V)

Logoed Items

Logoed items continue to market your business even when you're not around! They can make excellent gifts and don't have to blow your budget. As with printing your business cards, you may use a local company if there's one near you (this can stimulate cross-referrals and boost the local economy), or you may select an online company. (Hint: search under "promotional items.") Whatever you do, double- and triple-check for accuracy before you give your final approval.

You might be wondering what you can put your logo on. The answer is almost anything! Here's a partial list of ideas to get you started: t-shirts, polo shirts, sweatshirts, windbreakers, baseball hats, socks, shorts, gym or golf towels, golf tees, golf balls, luggage tags, clocks, pens, letter openers, Frisbees, key chains, first-aid kits, coffee mugs, travel mugs, trivets, puzzles, magnets, checkbook holders, notepads, mints, hot/cold packs, essential oils (through a distributor), supplements (through a distributor), lip balms, umbrellas, lanyards, highlighters, flashlights, kick sacs, stress balls, yo-yos, balloons, blankets, stuffed animals, fishing lures, coolers, stadium seats/cushions, rubber bracelets, cup holders, chocolates, beach balls, poker chips, Magic 8 Balls, monthly planners, USB drives, portfolios, cell phone cases, business card holders/cases, calculators, desk accessories, oven mitts, pocketknives, ice scrapers, tire gauges, chip clips, hand sanitizers, pocket mirrors, sun shades, bumper stickers, pins, awards, bandannas, mouse pads, paperweights, pedometers, blankets, and more!

Often there are discounts for bulk orders, and you can also look for close-out items to keep your costs down. Be creative and select items that will appeal to your ideal clients. Logoed items can be used as prizes for office contests, as giveaways at marketing events, as office "uniforms," and for retail sales. Always check your order upon arrival for accuracy, completeness, and quality.

Advertisements

Advertisements can appear in print, on radio, on the Internet, or on television. A few recommendations are:

• Know the state advertising rules, regulations, and guidelines for your profession.

• Make certain to include any required statements or disclaimers.

• Be ethical. Don't bait and switch—that is, don't promise something to get clients in the door and then not deliver on the promise.

• Know the advertising vehicles in your community and use the ones that will work best for you. For example, don't waste your money putting an advertisement in the newspaper when everyone looks to the local magazine for resources.

• Hire a professional to design your advertisement. Don't cut corners here—this is your professional image.

• Know your budget and aim for the highest quality advertisement you can obtain within that budget.

• Know your target audience and gear your advertisement to that audience. For example, if you develop a TV commercial geared toward working moms, you don't want it to air on weekdays while they're likely to be at work.

• Keep it simple and specific. Don't try to pitch your business as offering the perfect health solution for every person and every problem.

• A popular franchised advertising option for health and wellness practitioners is Natural Awakenings. Check www.naturalawakeningsmag.com to see if there's one in your area.

Large Events

Large events can bring the community together for a common cause and draw attention to your practice. Once again, a brief reminder: if you can't do a large event properly whether for reasons of budget, schedules, or logistics, don't do it . . . yet. Plan ahead, develop the resources, collaborate with others, and produce stellar events for your community! For some key considerations to keep in mind before, during, and after the event, please refer to the earlier section entitled Awareness Events. These ideas apply to the events discussed below, along with additional items for you to think about in each case.

Wellness Fair

A wellness fair can be approached in one of two ways. You can check with large local companies to see when their next employee wellness fair is being held and ask to participate. Or you can design and host your own wellness fairs within the community, held at your office or at another location. Organizing your own wellness fair can be a great option, especially if you have a Practitioner's Circle from which to draw vendors.

Depending upon the size of the fair and the venue, you may decide to charge vendors and attendees, or you may elect to keep it free of charge. You could also ask for donations at the door to donate to a charitable cause. Engage local healthcare practitioners to be vendors. Select them carefully and only use reputable providers. Be clear about what they can and can't do – for example, no hard-selling. Some provider options include:

- Medical doctors

- Optometrists

- Chiropractors

- Naturopathic doctors

- Acupuncturists

- Massage therapists

- Physical therapists

• A representative from the company's medical and dental insurance providers if this is a corporate event

• Dentists

• Fitness professionals (personal trainers, aerobics/yoga/Pilates instructors, and more)

• Nutritionists/dieticians

• Diabetes educators

• Local fire department/EMS

• Mental health professionals

• Nurse practitioners

• Blood drive/bone marrow drive

• Special providers as appropriate for the event (a doula, a La Leche League consultant, a Reiki master, an aromatherapist, local organic farmers, to name some)

Weight Loss Challenge

Overweight and obesity are tremendous challenges in the United States today, and they can lead to a multitude of health issues. Build on the success of TV's *The Biggest Loser* and other popular programs to help your clients achieve their weight loss goals. A Weight Loss Challenge can be done in your office, online, or on-site at another venue. You can work with an existing program such as Weight Watchers™, Jenny Craig™, Nutrisystem™, or Transitions™, or you can create your own program if you have the expertise. A word of caution: Don't attempt to create your own weight loss program if you lack the proper skills, knowledge, and training. Otherwise you could do more harm than good. If you've never done an event like this before, consider partnering with someone who has.

A weight loss challenge requires some special planning. Determine the criteria for participation. Do people have to submit "before" and "after" photos or an essay about their experience? What's the fee for participation, and what does it include? How many people can participate in the challenge? Can participants bring a partner or friend with them to join the challenge? Will there be multiple age or weight brackets? How will the winner be selected? How long will the program run, and what is its structure? For example, will participants do weekly weigh-ins but be responsible for their own weight loss activities? How will participants be supported in their endeavor? Will there be educational presentations or group training sessions? If so, when and where will they occur? Will everything be done online via a members-only website with resources and support, or will the challenge take some other form? Will participants be encouraged or required to use the services of an external website to log their food intake or exercise? These are just some of the questions to consider.

If there will be an educational component to the challenge, create the presentations, hand-outs, and other materials. As noted in previous sections, make sure these materials are clean, professional, accurate, and error-free. Line up any guest speakers and reserve the physical location for the meetings if necessary.

Will you solicit co-sponsors or host this event on your own? A wise choice of co-sponsor might be a local health club. As a co-sponsor, the club may be willing to donate the use of its space and/or the time of a personal trainer to facilitate the challenge. This is "free" advertising for the health club, and it helps your participants reach their goals. Will your challenge be affiliated with a local charity? For example, if your group reaches its weight loss goal, you and your co-sponsors will donate $1,000 to that local charity.

Are there going to be prizes or incentives for the winners? A gift certificate to a local store or a complimentary gym membership for the winner(s) would be appropriate options. If there are co-sponsors, consider having them donate prizes for the winner(s). It's *not* acceptable in most states for healthcare providers to offer cash as an incentive. If you're uncertain, check local, state, and professional regulations.

Finally, check with your professional liability insurance carrier to make sure you're covered for potential issues relating to this program, whether it's held on or off-site. If it's held on-site, also check your general liability insurance or consider adding an umbrella liability policy.

5K

A community 5K is an excellent way to encourage physical fitness and raise awareness and/or money for a specific cause. You may be able to gain assistance from local or national runners clubs in planning your 5K. The first time you organize an event like this, it can be a little overwhelming, but once you get the hang of it, it almost runs itself!

Before the 5K

Select your charity or cause and the theme. This can be done by you or by popular vote in the community. Be creative. Select a cause that resonates with you to make the event more appealing and enjoyable. Some interesting ideas are:

• **Zombie 5K/Run for Your Life:** (very popular in recent months!) Participants have three flags in their belts. They are chased by zombies who try to steal their flags. Runners who cross the finish line with at least one flag remaining in their belts have outrun the zombies!

• **Jingle Bell Run:** Participants must wear bells and other Christmas decorations.

• **Food Theme:** Instead of just water at the water stations, the participants can indulge in pita chips, fresh salsa, hummus, or dark chocolate-covered strawberries . . . whatever the theme may be!

• **Midnight Run:** Shake things up a little with a nighttime run. Make sure the route is properly lit to avoid injury and for security. This run could be combined with a New Year's celebration for added pizzazz.

• **Place-to-Place 5K:** The theme of this race is the course itself, which should highlight interesting, popular, or famous local places from start to finish. The places being featured (or other businesses along the route) could participate in co-sponsoring, helping to organize, or donating other kinds of assistance for the event.

• **5-Alarm 5K:** This race could benefit a local firefighter with a serious illness.

• **Hero Dash:** 5K meets an obstacle course in this race filled with physical feats firefighters face every day on the job.

• **Firefly Run:** A nighttime run with glow sticks and glow-in-the-dark tee-shirts. Another way to light up the night is to spray runners with neon glow water and light them with black lights.

• **Scottish Run:** Imagine kilts, bagpipes, and other Highland influences!

• **Color Run:** Participants start out in white tee-shirts and shorts. At each kilometer marker, they are splashed with a different color of non-toxic dyed cornstarch or with water colored with food dye. It creates almost a tie-dyed effect!

• **Dog Run:** Humans and their best friends run side by side to benefit the local animal shelter.

Select the date and time of the run, as well as the route. If you aren't a runner, ask a runner to help you map out an interesting route that's moderately difficult. You may want to map out an easier 3K walk for those who want to participate for fun. Determine the fees for sponsorship levels, participants, tee shirts, and anything else. Ask local businesses for donations or sponsorships. These can take the form of money, donated services, door prizes, tee shirts, water, or other supplies. (Refer to the previous section on Awareness Events for some key pointers on asking for donations!) The more supplies and services that are donated to the race, the less the 5K will cost. Some key donations to solicit include: Water (there are typically two to five water stations in a 5K), paper cups (two per runner per station is a good rule of thumb), race tee shirts, race website, graphic art or logo design for the race, and prizes for the winners.

Detailed logistical planning is imperative! Obtain official sanctioning through a runner's organization. In order to draw "professional" runners, you'll need to get the 5K officially recognized and log finish times for participants. It takes more work, but it can boost participation in your event. Contact the local police and fire departments. In many cities, a police presence is required in order to block off streets, and a fire department presence is required in order to have emergency medical services on-site. For the right cause, the police and fire departments may waive their fees. Also remember to check with your Town Hall to see if permits are needed.

What supplies and equipment will be needed? Who is responsible for those items? Where will the registration and award tables be setup? If there will be bathroom facilities, where will they be located? Where along the course will the water stations be located? Finally, obtain volunteers to help out before, during, and after the race with the setup, registration, water stations, finish line timing, and the awards table. Gather their contact information and tee shirt sizes for "Event Staff" labeled shirts. Confirm their participation prior to the race.

In addition to logistical planning, you must plan for the image and reputation of the 5K. This includes the image or logo design, the published handouts and other materials, the registration form, the runners' numbers, the award certificates, the press releases, the tee shirts, the route map, and the website. If the tee shirts aren't donated, an inexpensive resource is www.jakprints.com. You may wish to coordinate with other local fitness professionals and sponsors to propagate the event information. To help build momentum, perhaps a local gym could offer "couch to 5K" trainings. Don't forget to include a polished history of the charitable cause so people understand the reason for the race. Contact local media to arrange for promotion and/or coverage during the race.

Create checklists for the day of the event for each area (registration, volunteer coordination, water stations, finish line, awards table, and so on). See samples in Appendix C. Taking the time to create and update these checklists can help you delegate tasks and make sure everything gets done. Your goals are to have nothing fall through the cracks and to make sure your 5K goes off without a hitch!

In the days before the race, walk, run, or drive the course and note any changes or issues that need to be addressed before the runners hit the road. Does the course need to be modified for any reason? Immediately before the event, place arrows or other signage along the course so participants know exactly which way they are supposed to go. Make sure the water and safety stations are setup and clearly marked.

During the 5K

If you're not running in the 5K, you can use this time to check in with the water stations, the volunteers, the sponsors, and the registration/award table.

After the 5K

Distribute race results to local papers and running websites. Send thank-you notes to sponsors, vendors, and volunteers. Debrief with your staff and others to determine what could be changed to improve future races. Present the final check (after expenses) to the selected charity. Then begin planning your next 5K!

If you aren't a runner and don't know the first thing about 5Ks, don't despair! There are many national, state, and local organizations that can help bring you up to speed. The American Running Association (www.americanrunning.org) can provide an excellent overview of different races throughout the country. Running USA (www.runningusa.org) is also a great site for finding already-established events. You might use these sites to find an event in your area and contact the sponsor to ask for a little mentoring and guidance to help you bring your event to fruition. Finally, Road Runners Club of America (RRCA) (www.rrca.org) has an excellent website filled with information. RRCA supports the development of local clubs and events and has chapters all over the country. Contact your local chapter for assistance, or look on the RRCA website for educational and certification programs. The website also contains excellent resources such as printable PDFs of hot and cold weather running tips, etiquette for runners, and guidelines for safe events. Happy running!

Chapter 10:

Wrap-Up

Congratulations on making it to the end of this book! I hope it's given you helpful ideas for how to better position and market yourself and your practice in your community. While this book focused largely on external connection opportunities, please look for my next book, *Practice Excellence! An Integrated Approach to Creating a World-Class Healthcare Practice*. It's a continuation of the Community Connections series and delves into internal marketing opportunities and practice management concepts. Here are a few more pointers to help you in your journey:

• **Stay the course!** Community connecting is a process that can take time. Work on it a little each day, and you'll soon see the benefits.

• **Delegate!** If you're doing every step of every event by yourself, you'll rapidly get overwhelmed or burned out. Give your staff, co-sponsors, and volunteers responsibilities to handle. Not only will it take the pressure off of you, but it will help them to grow as well.

• **Prioritize!** You can't do everything at the same time. Make sure important or critical issues are handled first. Decide what things can wait to be addressed later.

• **Be organized!** In an organized office, the marketing virtually runs itself. If you aren't organized by nature, then ask for help! Hire a professional organizer and learn techniques from a pro.

• **Modify as needed!** If something isn't working, don't wait for it to fail. Modify and update the process or event so it can be successful.

• **Know your limits!** Don't spread yourself too thin. Operate within your limits. It's easier to add additional marketing opportunities into your schedule later if you find you have the time, energy, and motivation. It's better to start small and build. Don't cancel events that have been scheduled. This sends the message that you are unreliable.

• **Set yourself up to succeed!** When you're organized and passionate about what you do, when you've scheduled interesting and educational events to help your community, when you're energized and connected to your community . . . magic can happen!

• **Reflect!** After an event or connection opportunity, take time to reflect and solicit feedback. Consider what went well and what can be improved upon for next time. Take notes and follow through with any changes for subsequent events.

• **Remember why you do what you do!** A fabulous mentor of mine, Dr. Ron Boesch, always said that you need to "own your story." Never forget *why* you chose your profession. When times get tough, you can call upon this for strength.

In closing, I applaud you for your desire to connect with your community and grow your practice. Thank you for choosing this book to assist you. I truly hope it has given you ideas and motivation to stimulate success in your practice. If you know about an external Community Connections opportunity I didn't cover in this book, I encourage you to contact me at DrKelley@Dr-Kelley.com. Your suggestions will be added to future editions of this book and credited to you! I invite you to share your experiences and stories with me as we create a larger source of community for healthcare professionals. Finally, if you have any questions, or if there's anything I can do to help you promote health in your community, please don't hesitate to contact me!

Dr. Kelley S. Mulhern

www.Dr-Kelley.com

DrKelley@Dr-Kelley.com

###

I'm grateful you spent some of your valuable time to read my book! If you found it to be useful, please take a moment to submit a review at your favorite retailer.

Thank you!

Additional Resources

Appendix A: Sample Presentation List

Presentations on General Health Topics:

• **Boosting Your Immune System . . . Naturally** – Every year there is another infectious disease scare, and people feel increasingly disempowered to protect themselves. This class focuses on easy and simple ways that you can enhance the effectiveness of your immune system without drugs.

• **Non-Toxic Cleaning** – We all want a clean home, but often the cleaning supplies are more toxic than the mess! Learn tried-and-true non-toxic strategies to clean your home and protect your health.

• **The Energetics of Health** – Quantum physicists have known for decades of the existence of "subtle" or "energetic" bodies that are part of each human being. This class looks at the different energetic bodies and how they can affect our physical health. Special attention is given to alternative therapies that may help the subtle bodies to heal, thus promoting the health of our physical bodies.

• **Vaccines** – The decision to vaccinate your child is one of the most important decisions a parent can make. Unfortunately, most parents receive a one-sided view of vaccines and aren't given the ability to make a truly informed choice. This class explores both sides of the heated debate that continues to rage in our media.

• **Wellness 101** – This foundational class covers material that sets the stage for future classes. It includes a discussion of the changing definition of wellness, the false sense of security under which most Americans operate, and the top causes of declining health. Participants are encouraged to take a close look at their level of health and identify areas they could improve.

• **Understanding [fill in a specific health topic]** – This seminar explains [fill in the topic], including current statistics, risk factors, treatment, and prevention strategies for the layperson. [NOTE:

Topics could include heart disease, temporomandibular joint dysfunction (TMJD), arthritis, plantar fasciitis, osteoporosis, autism, diabetes, stroke, periodontal disease, shin splints, depression, anorexia, bulimia, hypertension, otitis media, cataracts, gastroesophageal reflux disease (GERD), celiac disease, or any other topic of interest to your clients.]

Presentations on Nutrition:

• **Nutrition Basics** – Eating well is no longer as simple as it used to be. During this program, we cover common misconceptions about nutrition and what the current research shows. Participants are provided with tips and techniques they can easily begin using right away to make a difference in their nutrition.

• **Deciphering Food Labels** – In this expansion of the Nutrition Basics class, participants learn how to read a food label and how to recognize common deceptions in advertising. Together we review food labels of common products as well as appropriate serving sizes.

• **Food Myths** – A continuation of our Nutrition Basics class, this workshop explores in more detail the misconceptions surrounding the issues of dairy, whole grains, and soy. The presentation includes a discussion of the Food Guide Pyramid and alternatives.

• **Genetically Modified Food** – "Franken-foods" are fast becoming the norm instead of the exception in our society. Learn what a **GM** food is, how to recognize it, and the impact GM foods can have on your body and on our economy.

• **The Glycemic Index Demystified** – As any person struggling with diabetes knows, knowledge of the Glycemic Index (GI) is critical to healthy living. Participants in this class will learn what the GI is and how to use it in their everyday lives to make better food choices.

• **The Skinny on Fats** – Dr. Adam Bordes created this lecture to help the average person make sense of all of the hype around fats. Which are "good fats?" Are the "bad fats" really bad? Do we actually need fats? Learn how to incorporate fats into your health program for optimal impact.

Presentations on Physical Health:

• **Body Basics: Physical Health** – The class covers the importance of motion in life. Various forms of exercise are discussed, including the population(s) for which they are most appropriate. Special attention is paid to familiarize participants with resistance bands and stability balls.

• **Office Ergonomics** – Employee health can dramatically affect the bottom line. This class provides employees with home- and office-based tips they can use immediately to improve their posture, their ergonomics, and their health.

Presentations on Emotional Health:

• **De-Stress and Revitalize!** – Participants will learn what stress is, its impact on the body, common causes of stress, and the connection between stress and disease. They will also learn how to start improving their body's ability to handle stress, and how to reduce the impact of stress on their body.

• **Forgiveness** – Often a controversial topic, forgiveness is nevertheless considered by most to be an integral component of a healing journey. This workshop explores a definition of forgiveness, when to forgive, when not to forgive, and how you know when the process is complete.

• **Goal Setting & Life Purpose** – The ability to set goals and having a sense of purpose are critical to one's success and overall sense of well-being. However, these are not skills commonly taught to us in school! This workshop focuses on three goal-setting techniques and helps participants find one that suits their personal style. It also looks at the concept of Life Purpose and how to discover yours!

• **Vision Board** – This workshop is commonly used as a follow-up to the Goal Setting & Life Purpose workshop. It combines creativity and fun with goal setting! Each participant goes home with their own personal visual expression of their goals, as well as an understanding of the process to use in the future to create additional vision boards.

Appendix B: Sample Post-Presentation Survey

[Your Letterhead]
[Current Presentation Topic]
Thank you for your attention and participation in today's class!
Please take a moment to help us help you and fill out this brief survey.

1. Did you find this presentation interesting?
❑ Yes❑ Not sure❑ No

2. Did you learn something new in this class?
❑ Yes❑ Not sure❑ No

3. Do you have any suggestions for how this presentation could be improved?

4. What other health topics are you interested in (please check all that apply)?
❑ Life purpose❑ Affirmations❑ Osteoporosis
❑ Vision boards❑ Journaling❑ Forgiveness
❑ Ergonomics❑ Diabetes❑ Arthritis
❑ Heart disease❑ Tobacco cessation❑ Injury/Inflammation
❑ Other: _____

Appendix C: Sample 5K Checklists

Registration Table

Blank Registration Forms
Tables
Chairs
Pens
Highlighters
Stapler and staples
Scissors
Tape
Safety pins
Donation jar
Registration packets:

- Runner numbers

- Hot Weather Running Tips

- Tee shirts

- Office information

- Topical analgesic sample

- Magnet with logo

- Pen with logo

Water Stations

Water
Paper cups
Plastic gloves
Tables
Trash cans
Trash can liners

Finish Line

Stopwatches
Time sheet
Pens/pencils

Awards Table

Table
Chairs
Electrical outlet
Surge protector
Extension cord
Computer
Printer
Award certificate paper
Pens
Age group awards sheet

Miscellaneous

Pacer
Route signage

Appendix D: Sample Letter to First-Time Sponsor

[Date]

[Name]
[Business Name]
[Address]

RE: 5K Run Donation

[Salutation – confirm name and spelling]:

Thank you so much for your willingness to provide [donation] for our upcoming charitable 5K run. As we discussed, the 5K is to benefit [charity, cause, or person]. [Brief history of cause and event].

The details of the 5K are as follows:

    Date:[date] RAIN OR SHINE
    Time: Registration & Packet Pick-up begins at [time] at [location]. Run begins promptly at [time]. Free tee shirts to the first 75 registrants [this or other details if appropriate].
    Course:[Describe the route the 5K will take. Include landmarks and street names.]
    Entry Fee:[fee] individual or [fee] per family/team of [number of members per team]
    Water: Total of [how many] stations.
    Parking:[location]

[Description of requested donation and how it was calculated, or description of their participation and what it entails.]

Once again, thank you so much for your generous donation! Your business name will go on the registration form and website as a sponsor [only include this statement if it is accurate. Otherwise, modify it as appropriate.] If you have any questions, please do not hesitate to contact me at [phone number].

Warm regards,

[Your name]

Appendix E: Sample Letter to Repeat Sponsor

[Date]

[Company Name]
[Address]

RE: [Donation]

[Salutation – confirm name and spelling]:

This letter is in regard to our 2nd annual 5K charity run to benefit [name of charity, cause, or person and a brief history]. Last year [Company Name] provided a generous donation of [donation] for the run, and we were hoping that you could do the same this year. As part of our community outreach program at [YOUR Company Name], we found out about [cause] and decided to help raise money for [it/him/her]. We are hoping that [Company Name] can donate [requested donation] for the event.

The 5K run is on [date] at [time]. The race starts and ends at [location]. [YOUR Company Name] and all of the supporting sponsors understand that if [Company Name] decides to donate [donation] for the event, the [donation] is to be used for the event only. [Donation] will not be sold before, during, or after the event.

Thank you so much for your time and consideration in this matter. [Company name] has a stellar reputation for community involvement, and we appreciate your support. Please feel free to call me at [phone number] if you have any questions.

Sincerely,

[Your Name]

Author Biography

Dr. Kelley S. Mulhern graduated from Logan College of Chiropractic in 2005 with a Doctorate of Chiropractic. She also holds Master's degrees in Public Health and Alternative Dispute Resolution, as well as Bachelor's degrees in Psychology, Sociology, and Human Biology.

For more than twenty years, she has worked in the healthcare industry in various capacities—as an employee, business owner, mentor, healthcare marketing consultant, professional speaker, and educator. When Dr. Kelley S. Mulhern first entered private practice, she couldn't find a book with marketing ideas appropriate for an independent healthcare business. This struggle provided the inspiration for the *Community Connections* series. She hopes this series will serve as a road map for healthcare practitioners working to build the practice and community of their dreams.

She currently lives in Saint Petersburg, Florida with her husband, Michael S. Mulhern, and their furry, four-legged child Kassi (former furry children: Phoenix, Sasha, Cree, Suki, Mira).

Together, Dr. Kelley and her husband Michael own and operate Thrive! Wellness Center based in St. Petersburg, Florida. Visit their website at thrivewellcenter.com. She and her husband also own and operate the online business Functional Wellness Docs. We help doctors, alternative medicine and holistic practitioners that practice Functional Medicine or Functional Wellness save time and money. Learn more at the website functionalwellnessdocs.com

Coming Soon!

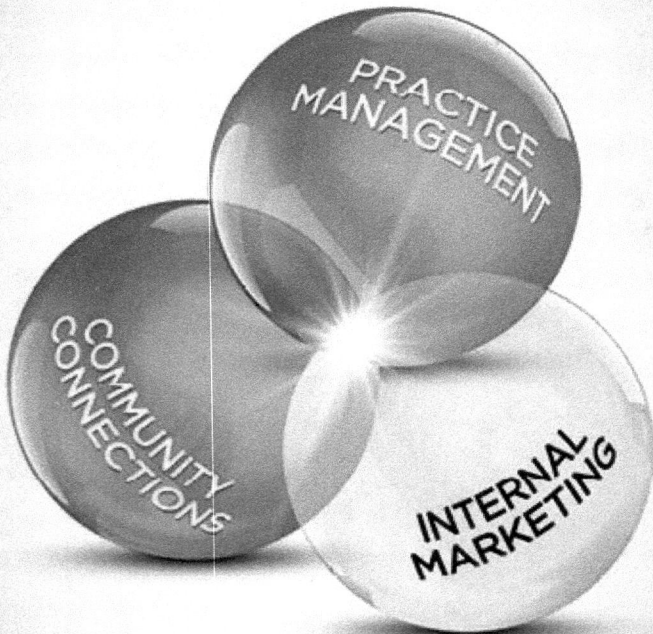

PRACTICE EXCELLENCE!

PRACTICE MANAGEMENT

COMMUNITY CONNECTIONS

INTERNAL MARKETING

An Integrated Approach To Creating
A World-Class Healthcare Practice

KELLEY S. MULHERN, M.S., D.C., M.P.H.

www.ingramcontent.com/pod-product-compliance
Lightning Source LLC
Chambersburg PA
CBHW050541280326
41933CB00011B/1678